An MP3, Belvaspata Angel Healing is available with the purchase of this book. It is a recording of Almine speaking the qualities and names of the angels in the language of the Infinite and has been created to assist in helping with pronunciation. To obtain your copy of the MP3 downloads, please visit www.belvaspata.org.

 Almine has also created an mp3 product, *Healing of the Angels*, in which she sings the names of the Angels of Divine Compassion and the blessings of the Infinite. This 60 minute musical healing experience is prefect for use during a healing session. To purchase a copy of the MP3 download go to:

http://alminewisdom.com/products/healing-of-the-angels

Belvaspata
Angel Healing

Second Edition

Almine

The Healing Modality of Miracles

Volume I

Plus: The Healing Methods of Enlightenment and
The Restoration of Inner Divinity

Published by Spiritual Journeys LLC

Second Edition August 2014

Copyright 2011

P.O. Box 300
Newport, Oregon 97365

US toll-free phone: 1-877-552-5646

www.spiritualjourneys.com

Cover Illustration by Dorian Dyer
www.visionheartart.com

Manufactured in the United States of America

ISBN 978-1-936926-92-3 Softcover

ISBN 978-1-936926-93-0 Adobe reader

Table of Contents

Part VII – Initiations: Self-Initiation into Belvaspata

Part VIII – Specialty Belvaspata Modalities

Book II – Kaanish Belvaspata – The Healing Modality of Enlightenment

Appendices

Foreword

In righting a wrong, we judge and divide. In acknowledging wholeness we uplift and inspire the underlying perfection to reveal itself. This miraculous healing modality, a divine gift to humanity, neither tries to heal nor fight disease. To do so would affirm the existence of such illusions.

Belvaspata replaces distorted matrices with clarity by emphasizing the expression of the pure luminosity and harmony that lies within each being. The stimulation of the true frequencies — the Song of the Self — in an individual creates self-healing by shattering the matrix within the body that holds disease programs in place.

Belvaspata has achieved rapidly growing acclaim worldwide as the modality of choice as its well-deserved reputation of success has spread among seasoned healers and newcomers alike.

Healing miracles have been reported from many countries. Interdimensional photography has captured the angels that come to assist practitioners in their efforts to expose the perfection and grace of existence.

Let the sacred work of bringing light to humanity spread around the world one person at a time. May Belvaspata practitioners everywhere be blessed in their ability to roll back illusions of despair and fear. Within their hands lie the gift of hope and the miracle of pure light and frequency.

Almine

Interdimensional Photograph of an Angel

Photograph taken by Raj Narinder in his garden

Dedication to Spiritual Healers

The way-showers of the world are my mission and my inspiration. My life is dedicated to you, the capstone of humanity. You are the ones who are not afraid to lay down old belief systems and open to the in-pouring of Spirit.

We have come through time and space together, from the first moments of created life, to meet upon this planet to turn the keys that will begin the journey home — back to the heart of God. I have been called forth for the specific task of touching the hearts of those who are the pillars of the temple, who uphold humanity by the light of their presence, both now and in the future.

It is you to whom I dedicate the teachings of healing. May your hearts recognize the many levels of light they impart. May you and I pull the Earth into an era of hope and peace and lay the path to a new tomorrow.

All my love,

Almine

Disclaimer

Belvaspata is not intended to diagnose, or to constitute medical advice or treatment. All healing takes place within self. Please follow all regulatory guidelines of your specific municipality in terms of assisting and working with others, even with their express consent. A physician or other healthcare professional should be consulted for any necessary medical attention.

Book I
Belvaspata Healing and Initiation Manual

PART I

Introduction

Belvaspata, the Healing Modality

Belvaspata, Healing of the Heart, is a sacred modality that heals with light and frequency. This healing method is a gift from the Infinite to the cosmic races to accommodate the changing laws of physics that took place as all life ascended into a new level of existence in August 2006. The language used is a very high cosmic language used by the Mother/Infinite Being and angels alike.

The use of Belvaspata heals as the frequencies of the sacred sigils are drawn to where they are most needed and takes into consideration changes that occurred in August 2006, altering the laws that govern all existence. (See The Sigil for Belvaspata on page 6.)

These laws changed as the frequencies within the cosmos raised us out of a cycle of existence in which polarity was the primary causation for cosmic movement. We had now entered a more elevated cycle of existence in which resonance became the basic moving force.

The most basic assumptions on which healers of all modalities had based their methods changed overnight. No longer did opposite energies attract, that healing energy could gravitate towards diseased energies. Now they would reject each other.

It became vital that healers begin to utilize light and frequency to dispel the illusion of disease, as under the changed cosmic laws, opposites would be attracted. ***The importance of working with Belvaspata is that light would now be drawn to illusion and frequency to distortion.***

Belvaspata, in the language of the Mother Goddess, means 'healing of the heart'. Whereas the primary purpose of previous cycles of existence was to seek perception (which is mind-oriented), the one we have entered has a different purpose. This cycle is like a blank canvas and challenges us to fulfill one primary purpose: **To create through the heart.**

The body of knowledge, which is Belvaspata, is a gift from the Mother/Infinite Being that we may fulfill the new purpose of life. It is here to help us create health, joy and happiness through the heart.

Belvaspata Updates following Recent Cosmic Changes

Cosmic changes also impact Belvaspata. Throughout creation there are various states of awareness and awakening and Belvaspata supports each of them for the benefit of all.

Polarity and duality no longer exist. All energy and power is now available to us and inseparable from us. It is no longer necessary to pulse between the poles to create energy. This also means that light and frequency, now unified, no longer are opposites that attract; all resources are immediately drawn to where they are most needed. This is the same for the Pairs of Emotions, Rays of Light, States of Being and Heart Energies discussed later in this book.

As the purpose of Belvaspata is to remove the illusion of all disease, to remove the illusion of distorted emotion and to remove the distortion of light, we can use Belvaspata as a tool to:

4

- see the perfection of all
- focus and enhance the perfection
- assist with the awakening of consciousness and to reveal the underlying perfection
- assist in the full expression of our being should it be blocked or not expressing fully

Belvaspata inspires the person (or a part of their body) to want to express at a higher level and/or to let go of patterns and behaviors held in the memory, thus releasing illusion and allowing fuller expression.

The ultimate gift of Belvaspata is to Align with the Song of Creation.

As an alchemical equation it reads:

Compassionate Support

+

Awakening from the Dream

=

Alignment with the Song of Creation

While doing Belvaspata, we envision the pristine perfection of all and know that the perfection already exists. In doing so, we assist and support the awareness of the perfection of all life. We look beyond the physical appearance and manifestation of disease to the existing underlying perfection; focusing on 'what is' — perfection — and removing the focus from 'what is not' — the imperfection.

The Sigil for Belvaspata

BELVASPATA
HEALING OF THE HEART

THE OVER-ALL ANGEL FOR BELVASPATA

Kelechnutvaveleshvispata

ANGEL SIGIL

Guidelines for Belvaspata Practitioners

- Maintain decorum of dress, manner and behavior. Strictly observe the confidentiality of all information that may be shared during a session.
- Provide a schedule of fees for your session to those you work with. Discussion of all fees should take place prior to a session.
- Offer adequate time for any questions or concerns prior to and possibly after a session. Individuals may require emotional support and reassurance before, during or after a session.
- A signed form of Release of Liability from those who receive sessions may be obtained prior to a session. This will be dependent upon individual preferences.
- Follow all legal guidelines for personal contact[1] with any person according to your individual municipalities and/or your state of residence.
- Remember that all healing takes place within the self. The information in this book is not intended to diagnose illness.
- When using Belvaspata to work on another, healing is made available to that individual or situation. It is not forced and is therefore readily available when all are receptive and ready. For this reason it is not necessary to obtain permission before using Belvaspata.
- Belvaspata may be done for yourself, another person, a situation or a location. It may also be done long-distance (see details in later section). Kriyavaspata[2] is specifically used for working with animals.
- A physician or other healthcare provider should be consulted for any necessary medical attention.

---

1 In the USA, licensed health practitioners are permitted by law to touch clients with permission of the client. Obtaining a valid minister's license (research on internet) may make it permissible to touch. Research and observe the legal guidelines that apply where you live.

2 See *Healing for Animals* www.kriyavaspata.com

Symbols versus Sigils

Before we start working with Belvaspata and the relevant sigils, we must first understand what a sigil is and the difference between a symbol and a sigil. We will then need to know the meanings of the sigils for this healing modality in order to properly understand and use them.

A symbol **represents** something, whereas a sigil **describes** something. When someone sees a BMW or a Mercedes symbol, it represents upper middle-class vehicles of quality and distinction. On the other hand, the symbol for a Rolls Royce or Bentley represents elite vehicles that speak of a privileged lifestyle of dignity and wealth.

So much is deduced just from one symbol. A Rolls Royce evokes images of walled estates, chauffeurs, enough and accustomed money where the symbol of a Ferrari will speak of more flamboyant taste.

Whereas symbols are common in our everyday world, the use of sigils is virtually forgotten. Even in mystery schools, their hidden knowledge eludes most mystics. Throughout the cosmos all beings of expanded awareness utilize sigils and it is only a few left-brain-oriented races that use symbols such as those in alphabets. An example would be the word 'LOVE' where we have combined four symbols (letters representing certain sounds) to make one symbol (the word that represents a feeling). But love is one of the building blocks of the cosmos, like space or energy.[3] It can also represent many different nuances within the emotion of love (which is the desire to include) and other types of dysfunctionality and degrees of need we mistakenly call 'love'.

---

3 Discussed in *Journey to the Heart of God*, The True Nature of the Seven Directions.

As we can see, the symbol or word can be very misleading since what it represents to one may not be what it represents to another. The sigil for love describes the quality or frequency of what is meant. It maps out the exact frequency of the emotion.

The sigil for someone's name would do the same. As the person or being rises in frequency, the sigil will change to reflect that. In the case of angels, even their names change. This is why the angel names or the goddess names have changed as the cosmos and Earth have ascended to a much higher frequency. In these higher realms the languages are also different and reflect the higher frequencies.

When a person has accomplished a major task within the cosmos pertaining to the agreement they made with the Infinite, they also receive a 'meaning' with its accompanying sigil. When a being is called to do a task meant for the highest good, that being will come if you have its name and meaning. The being absolutely must come if, in addition, you have the sigil for the name and meaning.

Having someone's sigil is like having that person's phone number.

Sigils not only describe what they represent, but are a means to communicate with what they represent.

The Significance of the Sigils

If all the other healing modalities are having their healing energy, and their symbols meant to produce healing energy repulsed, they are in fact producing the opposite of what is intended.

Because disease is distorted energy that repulses the natural healing energies (the trillions of little fragments of awareness that have been available to restore perfection), these methods would, in fact, produce disease.

On August 17, 2006, in order to prevent well-intentioned healers from doing harm, the Mother/Infinite Being took away the power behind healing modalities based on energy work. The power behind the previously used symbols was also removed. It is for this reason that the gift of Belvaspata was given to humanity.

The Mother/Infinite Being has given the sacred sigils of Belvaspata to us. As the cosmos grows in awareness these sigils are automatically upgraded and stay at an optimum level of efficiency. As sigils are packed full of awareness particles, it is the sigils given to us by the Infinite that contain the greatest amount of these particles.

As of the 21st of April 2008, Mother/Infinite Being changed the laws that governed sigils.

- Any attraction of resources are now immediate, exponential and non-linear.
- As the building blocks of life are upgraded during cosmic ascension, Belvaspata sigils will likewise be upgraded to attract the correct building blocks.
- *Light* and *love* are now inseparable, interconnected fields. When we speak of attracting light, light and love will both be attracted.

In November of 2013, a dramatic cosmic shift occurred that has never before taken place. In the previous paradigm (reality) of polarity and duality, we operated within the law of compensation; where one side of the pole gained and the other side lost. We are no longer within that previous reality of life where light and frequency were separate subatomic building blocks of life. They are now perfectly blended and integrated, and known as tonal luminosity.

Note: It is very important to remember that the sigils used in Belvaspata are sacred and should always be treated with respect and reverence. Should a drawing of a sigil fall on the floor, do not step over it or on it. When discarding Belvaspata sigils or angel names, they should be burned in a ceremonial manner with appreciation and gratitude.

The Significance of the Master and Grand Master Sigils

The Master and Grand Master Sigils are to be used only for the initiations of Master and Grand Master practitioners. This is because of the purpose/intent that is held within their power.

The sigils of Belvaspata have a hidden power behind the obvious. For a Level I and Level II practitioner, every time the sigils are used, they dispel the illusion of disease and the illusion of distortions found in light and frequency (emotion) everywhere. In other words, everywhere on earth, there is less disease each time they are used.

The Master Sigil and Grand Master Sigil extend this influence to affect not only life on earth, but also the whole cosmos. After having practiced the sigils regularly and above all internalized the Pure Emotions, the Rays of Light, States of Being and Heart Energies, Master and Grand Master practitioners become connected to the field of existence that spans the cosmos. Practicing Belvaspata therefore becomes a cosmic service, bringing healing to life everywhere.

Where great service is rendered, great rewards are given. The rewards in this instance are a strengthening of the previous sigils placed in centers of the Master's/Grand Master's body by 100 times. The second magnificent reward is higher consciousness for the master and greater silence of the mind. Mastery is defined as absence of dialogue in the mind, or silence of the mind; only masters have this option.

Disease as an Illusion

Initiates into Belvaspata must very clearly understand why disease and the false emotions of anger, fear, pain and protectiveness are at this point an illusion.

All healing is but the removal of illusion and is facilitated through the use of the sigils. One needs to remind oneself of this every time the sigils are used. To treat disease as a real adversary is to strengthen the illusion.

Almine relates that in 2005, the 'real' part, the indwelling life of disease, was removed. To demonstrate this she said that if she had put her pen on the table and one of the masters of the unseen realms removed the etheric or 'real' pen, it would no longer be real.

She could still pick the physical pen up and write with it. But some days she may not see it, and then one day, it will have disappeared altogether. It would, in fact, disappear even quicker if her thinking that it's on the table were to stop; if she knew it was now no longer real, but just an illusional shell without real life.

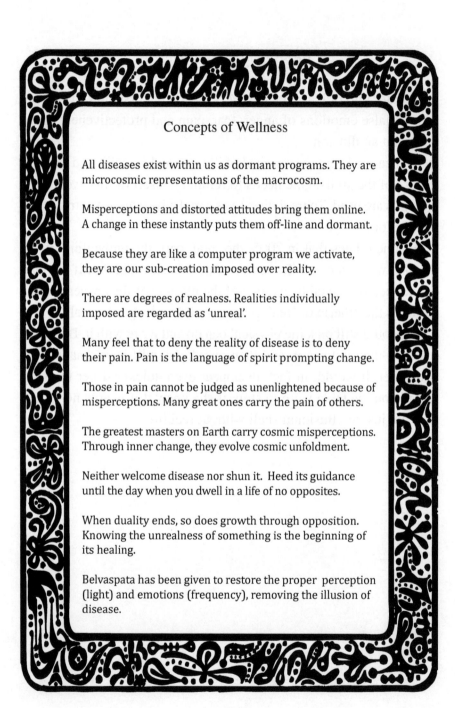

Concepts of Wellness

All diseases exist within us as dormant programs. They are microcosmic representations of the macrocosm.

Misperceptions and distorted attitudes bring them online. A change in these instantly puts them off-line and dormant.

Because they are like a computer program we activate, they are our sub-creation imposed over reality.

There are degrees of realness. Realities individually imposed are regarded as 'unreal'.

Many feel that to deny the reality of disease is to deny their pain. Pain is the language of spirit prompting change.

Those in pain cannot be judged as unenlightened because of misperceptions. Many great ones carry the pain of others.

The greatest masters on Earth carry cosmic misperceptions. Through inner change, they evolve cosmic unfoldment.

Neither welcome disease nor shun it. Heed its guidance until the day when you dwell in a life of no opposites.

When duality ends, so does growth through opposition. Knowing the unrealness of something is the beginning of its healing.

Belvaspata has been given to restore the proper perception (light) and emotions (frequency), removing the illusion of disease.

Belvaspata General Guidelines

1. Understand and know the difference between a symbol and a sigil.
2. The sigils of the healing qualities are drawn for both a session and for initiation. You do not have to memorize them. You can draw them in the air above or over the area of the body that is stated in the book or manual you are using, or a paper that you hold. You may also place the paper directly on the body and trace the sigil with your finger.
3. You do not sign/draw the angel sigils – look at them as you call their name either silently or out loud.
4. The sigils are drawn from left to right. Start at the upper left-hand corner and after that, the order is not crucial.
5. In some of the specialty Belvaspata modalities that are used to work with specific conditions, the sigils may be very complex. It is permissible to use one or several fingers held together to move across the sigil from left to right rather than drawing it. The left hand is receptive while the right hand represents understanding. You may use either hand according to your personal preference and intent. This method is only to be used for these very complex sigils and all other sigils (such as those in Level I, II Master and Grand Master Belvaspata) are to be signed/drawn.
6. Angel names may be called out loud or said silently as you wish and according to the preference of the person who is receiving Belvaspata. *Note: The hyphens used in the sigil qualities or angel names are added to assist with pronunciation.*
7. Using the *Power Source Wheel* (see page 54), place it above the head of the recipient during initiations or healing sessions to augment results.

8. Following cosmic changes, Level I and II Initiations may be done at the same time. There should be a 3 to 6 month interval between Level II and Master Level Initiations along with daily use of the sigils. Master and Grand Master Level initiations may now also be done at the same time. These guidelines apply to both self-initiation and to initiation with a Master or Grand Master of Belvaspata.

9. The intervals between initiations have been established to allow for the complete absorption and integration of these frequencies before advancing onto the next level. Be aware that the integration for some initiates may vary. This can depend on their use of the Belvaspata Sigils and their own readiness.

10. Further information for those who are new to working with healing modalities is provided in Appendix I at the back of the book.

11. Certification from the initiating Master or Grand Master may be provided for those who have received initiation into Belvaspata. *(See Belvaspata Certificates of Initiation in Appendices.)*

Note from Almine: You may charge the same fee as you would for other therapeutic modalities such as massage, for example. The only exchange I ask for from you and those you train is an acknowledgement that Belvaspata originated from me. If it would enhance the value of the modality in advertising, you may freely reprint any of the endorsements (or portions) from the back of my books.

PART II

Working with Belvaspata

How to Use Belvaspata

A Belvaspata Session

Work with the sigils that are appropriate to your level
of initiation. Remember that Master and Grand Master
Initiation Sigils are only to be used for initiation.

Opening every session

1. Sign/draw the sigil for *'Opening the Mind'* over the forehead
   once and say the sigil name. Call the Angel while looking at its
   sigil (do not draw the Angel sigil). Ask the Angel to place the
   sigil within the forehead.
2. Sign/draw the sigil for *'Opening the Heart'* over the heart once
   and say the sigil name. Call the Angel while looking at its sigil
   (do not draw the Angel sigil). Ask the Angel to place the sigil
   within the heart.
3. Sign/draw the sigil for *'Receptivity of the Body'* over the
   person's navel once and say the sigil name. Call the Angel
   while looking at its sigil (do not draw the Angel sigil). Ask the
   Angel to place the sigil within the person's body.

Remember the three steps above start every session
(See Opening Sigils on page 22)

4. One or more of Level II Initiation sigils may also be added after the above steps, at the discretion of the practitioner.

5. Ensure both you and the person you are working with are comfortable as you begin the session. You may place your hands either on or near the person's head, shoulders or feet (be aware if the laws in your area permit touching[4]).

6. Envision yourself expanding and expanding until you are as vast as the cosmos. Hold that expanded awareness for at least 20 minutes.

7. Now see the person you are working with expanding as well until you are both a consciousness blended as one with all that is. Hold that vision.

8. See the person's body within the vastness (just give it or the area of concern slight attention). Do not overly focus on 'the problem' but rather the existing perfection that already exists under the illusion of disease — maintain the expansion.

9. Bring the pre-determined pair of emotions[5] that you have chosen for the session, into your awareness. Feel them ripple throughout all of the cosmos. Stay expanded — do not draw the sigils yet.

10. Maintain the state of expansion throughout the session. Only pull your awareness slightly back before you begin to draw the sigils you have been guided to use. If indicated, draw the sigil over the specific part of the body mentioned.

---

4 In US licensed health practitioners are permitted by law to touch clients with the permission of the client. Obtaining a valid minister's license (research on internet) may make it permissible to touch. Research and observe the legal guidelines that apply in your area/country.

5 When doing a simple session, you may wish to use only one pair of Emotions, specific to the issue or body part that is affected. An example would be to use the sigils for the pair 'Passion and Joy' for circulatory issues. It is beneficial however to draw all of the Sigils for the Pairs of Emotions for any first session as it restores the emotions to purity and clarity, which assists with all healing.

11. Any sigils that are appropriate for your specific level of mastery and that you feel are necessary for the session may be used, such as: the Pairs of Emotions, Rays of Light, Sigil for Self-love, advanced sigils, etc. *(See pages 42-44, 47-52, 62-64 and 70-80.)* Always draw both sigils of a pair as this promotes balance.

12. Specialty Belvaspata modalities may be added to a basic session. For example, you could add part or all of Kaanish Belvaspata, following the basic session and prior to closing the session. An exception to this is Belvaspata of the Song of Self, which is to be done prior to a basic session.

13. Always end a session by signing the sigils for love, praise and gratitude over the heart area or the entire body — this materializes the healing intentions and pulls awareness in.

14. Advise the person to drink plenty of water and rest as needed following a session. Some may need to ground or center themselves before returning to activities such as driving, etc. You may offer the person the opportunity to contact you if necessary.

Note: Strive to create a warm, comfortable and relaxing environment. Gentle background music, soft lighting, blankets and pillows can assist. Keep outside noise to a minimum and avoid any interruptions from phones, pets, etc.

Sigils for Opening a Session

These are the Level I initiation sigils that are
used to open a session or an initiation.

Quality	**Angel Name and Sigil**

Bla-utva-pa-ta
(Opening the Mind)
Draw over the forehead

Rutsetvi-uru-bach

Kru-vech-pa-uru-rek
(Opening of the Heart)
Draw over the heart

Iornumubach

Kel-a-vis-ba-vah
(Receptivity of the Body)
Draw over the navel

Tru-ararir-pleva

Sigils for Closing a Session

These sigils are used to close each session and initiation.
They may be drawn over the heart area or over the entire body.

Praise

Love

Gratitude

How to Use and Draw/Sign a Sigil

The following is an example of using a Level I sigil *(see page 26).* In this case, we are using the sigil for a session and not an initiation.

When using a Level I sigil for opening a session:

Step 1. Draw the sigil **1 time** over the forehead as indicated.

Step 2. Call (say) the quality of the sigil either out loud or silently **1 time** in Mother's language. Example of the quality of this sigil is: **Bla-utva-pata.**

Step 3. Look at the sigil for the angel name and call (say) the angel name either out loud or silently **1 time** in Mother's language. (It is not necessary to draw the sigil for the angel name.) An example of the angel name for this Level I sigil is: **Rutsetvi-uru-bach**. Ask the angel to place the sigil within the forehead (or as the specific sigil indicates).

Note: Some sigils, such as the 12 Pairs of Emotions and Rays of Light, have only one sigil, which is the sigil for the quality. Draw the sigil and call (say) the quality and the Angel or Lord's name out loud or silently. Use the sigil(s) over appropriate areas, as indicated or as you are guided if specific areas are not indicated. Always draw both sigils of a pair as this promotes balance.

See the example below of one of the 12 Pairs of Emotions, a set of paired sigils.

+

Creativity/Angel name:
Velesvruchba

genitals,
reproductive organs

−

Pleasure/Angel name:
Prubechbanatruva

Illustration of Level I Sigil

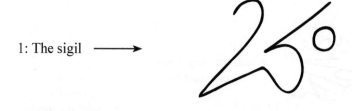

1: The sigil   ⟶

2: Area over which   ⟶   *To be drawn over the forehead*
to draw the sigil

3. Quality (meaning) of the   ⟶   **Bla-utva-pata**
sigil in the Mother's
Language

4. Intent of sigil   ⟶   *For opening of the mind*

By the power of this sigil which I hold in my hand, I call in the Angel

5. Angel name in the   ⟶   **Rutsetvi-uru-bach**
Mother's Language

6. Look at the sigil for the angel as you call the angel's name

Angel Sigil

Belvaspata Long-Distance Sessions

Belvaspata healing is effective whether done long-distance or in person. Sometimes an absentee or long-distance session is the most convenient way of working with another person. You may offer the person the opportunity to speak to you prior to the session to determine their reason and intent for it.

1. Follow the same guidelines as for a session done with someone in person. (The person may be advised to lie down during the session in a quiet location, where they will be undisturbed but this is not required.) The session is done with intent to hold the expansion of awareness, to bring the person into this expansion and to work with the sigils for their specific situation.
2. Do not use a teddy bear or other 'proxy' to represent the person that you are working with while doing a long-distance session. Remember that we are not 'sending energy.' Belvaspata works with light and frequency and is attracted to where it is most needed.
3. The person may also be phoned after a session as both parties may have information to share.
4. Advise the person to drink plenty of water and rest as needed following a session. Some may need to ground or center before returning to activities such as driving, etc. You may offer the person the opportunity to contact you if needed.

Belvaspata and Self-Healing

Self-Healing for Belvaspata Practitioners

All self-healing is done by accessing our true self, the One Being, the All.

To do this:

- Go to the largest possible expansion of Self.
- Feel that which you want to access WITHIN THE SELF
- You can now access ALL without limit as ALL is within you

When doing a session on yourself the format for self-healing is the same as for working with another person. Draw the sigils in the air and ask the angels to place them in the appropriate areas of the body.

Working on oneself is the greatest gift that one can give oneself. All healing, whether done for another or for oneself, is a blessing to all life and assists in elevating all to a higher level, as the perfection is further revealed. There is, in truth, only One Being.

Images of practitioner's hand healed within a few days using Belvaspata

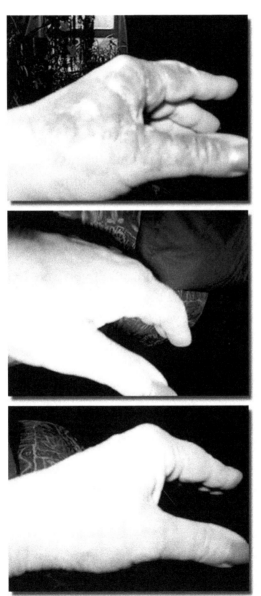

Belvaspata Questions and Answers

Q. How was this healing modality received by Almine?

A. Almine was explaining to a healer in her class in Ireland why a specific energy-based modality wouldn't work when she saw a group of butterflies come through the window and turn into sigils as they flew over the healer's right shoulder and into Almine's forehead. She then went to a flipchart and started writing the sigils and accompanying words as rapidly as she could. Class ended at that point, but in her hotel room, sigils, words and information came through the night until 7a.m. the next morning.

Q. Does one have to be initiated to use the sigils and if so, how?

A. Absolutely, one has to be initiated. If you were to ask an initiate, they will be able to describe how profound the initiation experience is as the sigils are conveyed from a Belvaspata Master. Students need to integrate and internalize the 12 Pairs of Emotions for Level I, the 16 Rays of Light for Level II, the 12 Pairs of States of Being for Master Level and the 12 Pairs of Heart Energies for the Grand Master Level, prior to receiving their initiation into each of these levels of Belvaspata.

Q. This healing method was a gift from the Creator Goddess/Infinite, through Almine to each of us who are initiated into the Master and Grand Master Levels. Why is it important to honor the Source, or lineage, of this gift when we use it for healing sessions or when giving initiations?

A. As we acknowledge and honor the Source, we connect with the lineage of power and purity directly from the Infinite, to Almine and through all others who are initiated before us. The more we expand our hearts through the attitudes of Love, Praise and Gratitude, the more we open to the fullness of the power of Belvaspata. We may feel this power come into us as a physical sensation such as energy moving through one's body, warmth, coolness, tingling, a feeling of excitement, etc.

The Belvaspata healing modality is a gift from Mother/Infinite Source, through Almine and as such reflects the Divine Perfection and is supported by the Angels who work with Belvaspata and its sigils.

Q. Can the time frame for receiving the initiations be reduced?

A. When attending a retreat with Almine, the waiting period between initiations is waived. This is due to the expansion and high frequency levels attained during the retreat. All other initiations must maintain the minimum time periods between initiations. This allows full integration and absorption of the frequencies to occur prior to being initiated into the next level. Some initiates may need longer for this than others.

Q. Having received Level I Belvaspata, is it okay to do healing sessions on others and myself? What benefits does one receive?

A. Yes, Level I masters may use Belvaspata on themselves or others. Through the interconnectedness of all life, the healing frequencies of Belvaspata automatically go where they are most needed so all life benefits. In this way one is of greater service. Through the archetype principle — that which we accomplish for ourselves is also accomplished for all.

Q. What is the significance of the tenth chakra?

A. The Lemurian name for 'ten' is 'Lahun'. This means *One in All* and *All in One*. The 'law of the one' the Atlantean mysteries taught about also pertains to the mystical principles of the 10th chakra. As an initiate becomes an adept and later a master (all three of these phases are still in ego-identification), 12 chakras open.

During subsequent evolutionary stages such as god consciousness and ascended mastery, the tenth chakra (about the size of a dinner plate, often depicted as a sign of enlightenment above the head in Egyptian and Sumerian art), 10" above the head, enlarges. It continues to grow bigger and bigger until it encloses all other chakras during the ascended mastery stage. *All is now One,* and *One is in all.* By initiating it last, this process is activated.

Q. Have any changes occurred in the sigils or the positions of the Lords, Gods and Goddesses of Belvaspata since it was first received?

A. As the cosmos continues to ascend, grow and evolve, so also will the sigils and the positions of the Angels, Lords, Gods and Goddesses of Belvaspata change and rise to reflect the higher levels of consciousness. This means that they will always retain their purity and remain at their most potent.

Q. I know it is important to honor the sacred nature of Belvaspata. If I make extra copies of Belvaspata initiation sigils or angel names or use on business cards, flyers, etc — what is the best way to discard them?

A. It is always wise to trust our heart and our feelings to direct our course of actions. Working with Belvaspata removes distortions and makes our guidance ever clearer.

You are correct to remove any Belvaspata sacred material from public sites and never to throw any of it into a wastebasket. Always handle the sigils and angel names in a sacred manner. They should never be placed on the floor or have other objects casually placed on top of them. Sigils should always be handled as one would handle any other sacred object, with the care and dignity befitting their holy nature. In this way we honor the Infinite, Almine, Belvaspata (which is the Infinite's gift to us), ourselves and All.

When discarding Belvaspata sigils or angel names, they should be burned in a ceremonial manner with appreciation and gratitude.

Q. If we accept payment for this sacred healing modality, aren't we blocking the flow of supply?

A. Every time a first or second level healer uses the sigils, a portion of the Earth and its population are healed. Because the Master Sigil connects the master healer to the cosmos, every time a master healer heals with these sigils, it affects the cosmos. The Grand Master sigil assists with preparing the physical body for immortality and to clear old programming. How can any amount of money ever be adequate repayment? You will still be leaving the cosmos in your debt.

PART III

Level I and Level II Belvaspata

Level I Belvaspata

In preparation for Belvaspata's Level I initiation, the initiate must study and internalize the twelve frequencies (emotions) that comprise the twelve frequency bands of the cosmos. They are not only necessary for initiation but also form an integral part of a Belvaspata session.

As we revisit these frequencies we will feel and understand them more fully.

- They will become stronger and deeper within us.
- It will become easier to experience and generate them as part of a session.
- We will live them more fully.
- Should the old discordant emotions of pain, anger, fear and protectiveness surface, we can instantly move into the new.
- The more we live them, the more they are available for others.

When working with a pair of sigils for the Emotions, always draw both sigils of the pair. These emotions do not have a separate angel and quality sigil.

For a simple session, you may want to use only one or a couple of pairs of emotions and their relevant sigils. It is however extremely beneficial to use all twelve pairs, especially for an initial Belvaspata session, as it balances the emotions. Always follow your own guidance.

Further information is given on these emotions in the chapter, *Preparing for Initiation.*

The 12 Pairs of Emotions

(-)   **(+)**

1) **Trust**   **Love**
The desire to surrender   The desire to include
(replaced fear)

2) **Peace**   **Inspiration**
The desire to be at ease, to feel   The desire to inspire and to
at home (replaced protectiveness)   be inspired (replaced anger)

3) **Pleasure**   **Creativity**
The desire to be delighted   The desire to create

4) **Acknowledgement**   **Empathy**
The desire to see perfection   The desire to connect

5) **Receptivity**   **Generosity**
The desire to receive   The desire to give

6) **Beauty**   **Encouragement**
The desire to be uplifted   The desire to encourage and
                                 to be encouraged

7) **Assimilation**   **Communication**
The desire to integrate   The desire to express

8) **Joy**   **Passion**
The desire to live   The desire to know

9) **Fun**
The desire to revel

Achievement
The desire to excel

10) **Contentment**
The desire to retain

Enlightenment
The desire to enhance and to
to be enhanced (replaced
pain)

11) **Humor**
The desire to be amused

Empowerment
The desire to be of service

12) **Satisfaction**
The desire to be fulfilled

Growth
The desire to expand

Note: Due to the changes that took place in the cosmos during August 2008, which brought about the healing of duality and polarity and the ending of linear time, the emotions no longer pulse one another. The Emotions now form a unified field that contains the qualities of all emotions with each being a specific emphasis of the whole. It is still therefore very important to understand the unique qualities within each of the emotional pairings and how they inspire one another.

The Twelve Bands of Emotions

In the previous cycle light formed the matrix of the cosmos, while emotion and awareness moved. Then, rings of emotion formed the matrix and light moved within it. Now omnipresent awareness permeates everything within the cosmos.

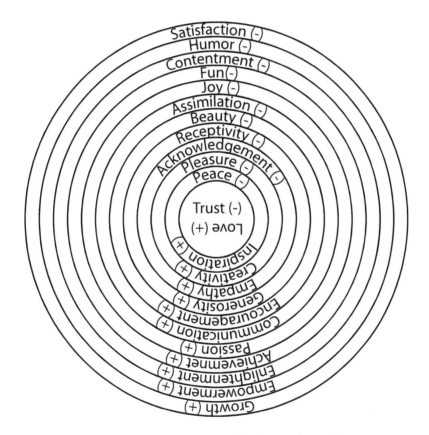

Each band represents a paired set of emotions.

The Sigils of Level I Belvaspata
The Sigils of Love

(also known as the 12 Pairs of Emotions)

1. Love (+)

Trust (-)

Uses:
Use for obesity
and excess muscle
and weight

Angel:
Perech-pri-parva

Angel:
Trues-sabru-varabi

---

2. Inspiration (+)

Peace (-)

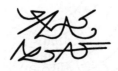

Uses:
Use in areas of
rash, redness or
inflammation

Angel:
Kriavat-bishpi

Angel:
Pele-nanvabruk

---

3. Creativity (+)

Pleasure (-)

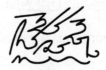

Uses:
Genitals and
Reproductive Organs

Angel:
Veles-vruchba

Angel:
Prubechba-natruva

---

4. Empathy (+)

Acknowledgement (-)

Uses:
Injuries

Angel:
Felvi-respi-uhuru-vak

Angel:
Tre-uch-vara-vaar

---

5. Generosity (+)

Angel:
Teshvinechspi-urarat

Receptivity (-)

Angel:
Nenhursh-brechbravit

Uses:
To reduce blood
pressure

---

6. Encouragement (+)

Angel:
Kletsut-vesba

Beauty (-)

Angel:
Nunberesh-nuk

Uses:
Pancreas, liver
and gallbladder

---

7. Communication (+)

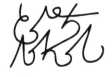

Angel:
Araragatveshpi

Assimilation (-)

Angel:
Nun-heresh-vispi

Uses:
Lungs

---

8. Passion (+)

Angel:
Gelkrig-sutvra-bararech

Joy (-)

Angel:
Travi-usbava

Uses:
For poor circulation

---

9. Achievement (+)

Angel:
Gele-vish-tra-va

Fun (-)

Angel:
Pru-eshbi-klechvaha

Uses:
Throat, thyroid

---

10. Enlightenment (+)

Angel:
Grunachberesvik

Contentment (-)

Angel:
Kletsatvarabuch

Uses:
Use for pain

---

11. Empowerment (+)

Angel:
Bu-esbi-klechnatra

Humor (-)

Angel:
Veluchvespri-rekva

Uses:
Digestive tract,
elimination, kidneys
and adrenals

---

12. Growth (+)

Angel:
Trubi-kluvespraha

Satisfaction (-)

Angel:
Nechtruavar

Uses:
Bones, fractures,
muscles and joints

Level II Belvaspata

Level II Belvaspata uses the 16 Rays of Light with each ray having its own color and quality. They are studied in preparation for Initiation (see chapter *Preparing for Initiation* for more information on the Rays of Light). It's beneficial to review them occasionally and further study their qualities. As with the 12 pairs of Pure Emotions, the more we understand and appreciate the qualities within these Rays of Light, the more they are available for all. These sigils are called the Sigils of Light.

16 Rays of Light

1. The Root	9. Bliss
2. Faith	10. Perception
3. Balance	11. Presence
4. Abundance	12. Hope
5. Wisdom	13. Mastery
6. Mercy	14. Discovery
7. Diversity	15. Power
8. Energy	16. Truth

The first Ray of Light, the Root, is always held by the Infinite. When using any of the Rays of Light, the Root is always used.

The Sixteen Rays of Light

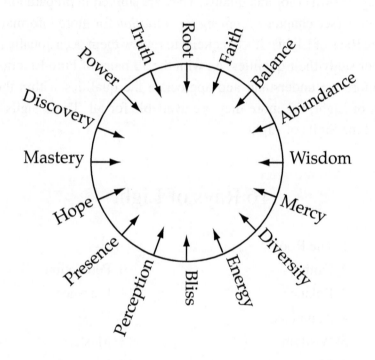

The Sigils of Level II Belvaspata
Sigils of Light

1. Name of Ray: **Root**

Lord's name: **Herhut-brasta**

Uses:
Always use in conjunction with other sigils of light

2. Name of Ray: **Faith**

Lord's name: **Belblutvakreshbi**

Uses:
Systemic illness

3. Name of Ray: **Balance**

Lord's name: **Kluch-nenuvit**

Uses:
Ears, throat, nose

4. Name of Ray: **Abundance**

Lord's name: **Petrevusbi**

Uses:
Prostate, rectum

5. Name of Ray: **Wisdom**

Uses:
Pineal, hypothalmus

Lord's name: **Gelviveshbi**

6. Name of Ray: **Mercy**

Uses:
Spine, occipital
area, base of skull

Lord's name: **Truavar**

7. Name of Ray: **Diversity**

Uses:
DNA, chromosomes,
memory

Lord's name: **Pluakbar**

8. Name of Ray: **Energy**

Uses:
Blood sugar,
blood purification

Lord's name: **Trechvarvulesbi**

9. Name of Ray: **Bliss**

Uses:
Cellular light, oxygen
and pH of cells

Lord's name: **Besbrakva**

10. Name of Ray: **Perception**

Uses:
Eyes, pituitary, 3rd eye

Lord's name: **Telenuchvraha**

11. Name of Ray: **Presence**

Uses:
Legs and feet

Lord's name: **Klechsavra**

12. Name of Ray: **Hope**

Uses:
Heart, circulation

Lord's name: **Telerutskrava**

13. Name of Ray: **Mastery**

Lord's name: **Brishnavak**

Uses:
Brain, clarity
of thought

14. Name of Ray: **Discovery**

Lord's name: **Verebisma**

Uses:
Tongue, teeth
and tonsils

15. Name of Ray: **Power**

Lord's name: **Veruch-mavaheshbi**

Uses:
Skull, scalp and hair

16. Name of Ray: **Truth**

Lord's name: **Petluch-vraha**

Uses:
Arms, shoulders,
elbows, hands
and wrists

Additional Sigils for

Level I and Level II Practitioners

Sigil for Presence
(This sigil may be used for the treatment of various cancers)

Kurash-berech-verespi   Angel: **Bilach-uvrespi-spaurach**

Sigil for combining frequency and light into one interconnected field
(This sigil can be used anytime imbalance exists)

Kirasta-elech-bruk   Angel: **Ninhursta-uvechvi**
(female)

Sigil for Emotional Health
(This sigil can be used for emotional health and depression)

Angel: **Nechvikrechbar**

Sigil for Self-Love
(This sigil can be used for enhancing and healing with self-love)

Kluhavespi-sta-unag

Angel: **Kiritre-anuch** (female)

Sigil for Archangel Micheal
(The Guardian of Sacred Space)

New Name: **Ephrimvael**

Meaning: **The Guardian of the Sacred**

Sigil for Silencing the Mind
(To silence the inner dialogue of the mind)

Kanig-vishva-heresvi

The Infinite's Sigil

Pi-helaa Stanuchvi

Kaa iri vish esta, na nut klavaa haruhash
Wherever life exists, there perfection is also

Note: The Infinite's Sigil is the symbol for connection to Source. It can be used as a meditation or focus tool to connect to the Infinite. It may be posted in living areas, walls of your room or house, under your mattress or table that you use for Belvaspata sessions as it contains a specific frequency. It does not have a specific purpose as a sigil for doing Belvaspata sessions or initiations.

The Power Source Wheel

The use of the Power Source Wheel will augment
results. It contains three languages that were used by
the Infinite during different creational cycles.

Master Level and
Grand Master Level Belvaspata

PART IV

Master Level and
Grand Master Level Belvaspata

Master Level Belvaspata

Master Level Belvaspata requires that you understand and internalize the frequencies of the States of Being. Along with the information on the States of Being are sigils that each have a specific healing intent. It is also beneficial to revisit them occasionally to gain a greater awareness of the qualities of these States.

As with the sigils for the 12 Pairs of Emotions, both sigils should be drawn. Each pair of States of Being also has an angel sigil; this sigil does not need to be drawn. Look at it as you call the angel by name.

The Master Level Sigil is only to be used for initiation. It is not to be used as part of a healing session.

The States of Being

(+)	(-)
Praise	Glory
Exploration	Harmony
Gratitude	Guidance
Discernment	Transparency
Understanding	Reflection
Embrace	Ecstasy
Manifestation	Inevitability
Oneness	Contentment
Integration	Evolution
Play	Flexibility
Perception	Power
Retention	Conductivity

Further information on the States of Being is given in the chapter *Preparing for Initiation.*

The Twelve Pairs of States of Being

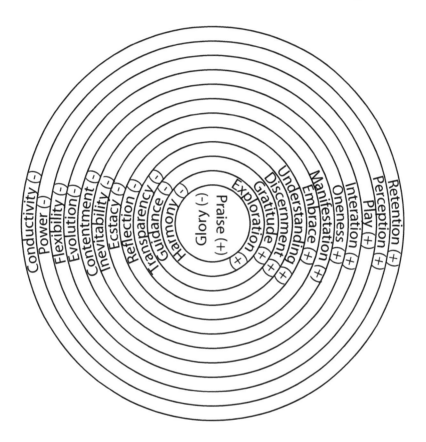

How the Emotions and States of Being Surround the Body

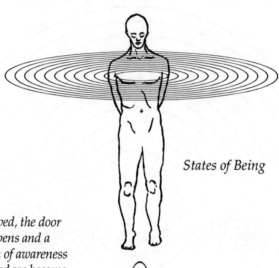

States of Being

When fully lived, the door in the heart opens and a feminine form of awareness is produced and we become co-creators

Emotions

How the Emotions and States of Being Intersect

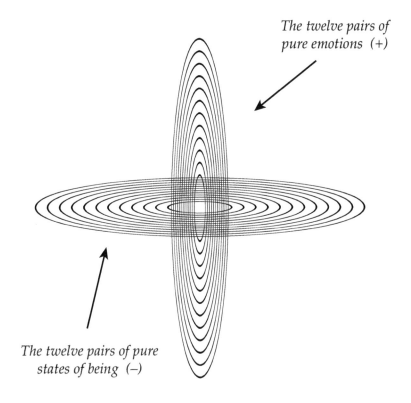

The twelve pairs of pure emotions (+)

The twelve pairs of pure states of being (−)

The Sigils of Master Level Belvaspata
The Sigils of The States of Being

1. **Praise (+)**   **Glory (-)**   **Use**

Angel:
Kuluheshpiuvrata

To increase awareness by infusing the blood stream with awareness particles.

2. **Exploration (+)**   **Harmony (-)**   **Use**

Angel:
Grustervirabach

To clear neuro-pathways and enhance the perception of subtle information.

3. **Integration (+)**   **Evolution (-)**   **Use**

Angel:
Kruapretparva

To balance the tones of all the bodies of man.

4. **Discernment (+)**   **Transparency (-)**   **Use**

Angel:
Nunheshbielstuavet

For the integration of all nine levels of light as information.

Sigils of The States of Being

5. **Understanding (+)**   **Reflection (-)**   **Use**

For the excretion
of higher
hormones to
evolve the
physical body.

Angel:
Brashechnetvetparva

---

6. **Play (+)**   **Flexibility (-)**   **Use**

For the evolving
of the DNA to
the next stages of
evolution.

Angel:
Gertraskuvaelenustraberechnit

---

7. Perception (+)   **Power (-)**   **Use**

Opening the
doorways of
potential.

Angel:
Pelenichvrausetbi

---

8. **Embrace (+)**   **Ecstasy (-)**   **Use**

For the
connection with
the Infinite
Mother to be
established.

Angel:
Grustachvauveshbi

Sigils of The States of Being

9. **Manifestation (+)**	**Inevitability (-)**	**Use**
Angel: **Gelstraubechspi**		For the expression and interpretation of full potential.
10. **Gratitude (+)**	**Guidance (-)**	**Use**
Angel: **Vertlusbraveparhut**		For the awakening of the inner hearing and clairaudience.
11. **Oneness (+)**	**Contentment (-)**	**Use**
Angel: **Sutbiuvechbiklausetvaruach**		For the removal of any obstacles to clairvoyance and the awakening of second sight.
12. **Retention (+)**	**Conductivity (-)**	**Use**
Angel: **Viresklachbirestna**		For the release of any blockages of perception in the higher bodies.

Grand Master Level Belvaspata

Introduction

Belvaspata's first three levels are meant to beneficially impact the physical, etheric, emotional, and mental bodies of beings only; Level II affects the four lower bodies of the planet. At the Master Level, the four lower bodies of the cosmos are also affected by the sigils.

The Grand Master Level affects the spiritual emotional, spiritual mental and spirit bodies of all. It promotes the coming together of life in the more subtle and physical levels of existence. This level of Belvaspata also removes obstructions that interfere with the opening and blossoming of the many new enhancements now found in that unique archetype, man.

The Grand Master Level is the level for the immortality of the body. It is designed to release new hormones and open the higher capacities of the endocrine system. It connects the individual with assistance from the highest levels within the cosmos. It draws in additional angelic presences into our lives and brings clarity of mind and purity of heart as the pathways of light are cleared within the seventh body or spirit body. As it does so, it clears the cosmic pathways and removes old programming of suffering.

The frequencies of the Grand Master Level were born as the Pure Emotion and the States of Being 'pulsed' with one another. This is no longer necessary, as all are now part of the unified field. These frequencies do not have their own specific healing sigils but it is important to revisit them so that they are understood and felt more intensely. (See chapter on *Preparing for Initiation*.)

The Heart Energies

1. Ecstasy (+)   +   Embrace (-)   = Divine Compassion
2. Insight (+)   +   Appreciation (-)   = Reverence
3. Inspiration (+)   +   Love (-)   = Pure Creativity
4. Truth (+)   +   Clarity (-)   = Absolute truth
5. Manifestation (+) +   Gratitude (-)   = Impeccability
6. Rejoicing (+)   +   Praise (-)   = Celebration
7. Harmony (+)   +   Wisdom (-)   = Timing
8. Fulfillment (+)   +   Presence (-)   = Focus
9. Growth (+)   +   Balance (-)   = Strength
10. Evolution (+)   +   Surrender (-)   = Grace
11. Discovery (+)   +   Awareness (-)   = Clarity
12. Acceptance (+)   +   Allowing (-)   = Harmlessness

This level of Belvaspata is accompanied by a set of 10 sigils that each relate to and are drawn over a specific area of the body. They may be used on their own or in conjunction with other sigils in a session. Placement of sigils is shown on page 74. If they are being used on their own for a session — always start with the Opening Sigils and end with the Closing Sigils.

The Grand Master Level Sigil is only to be used for initiation. It is not to be used as part of a healing session.

Creating the Twelve Heart Energies
How the Emotions and States of Being Intersect

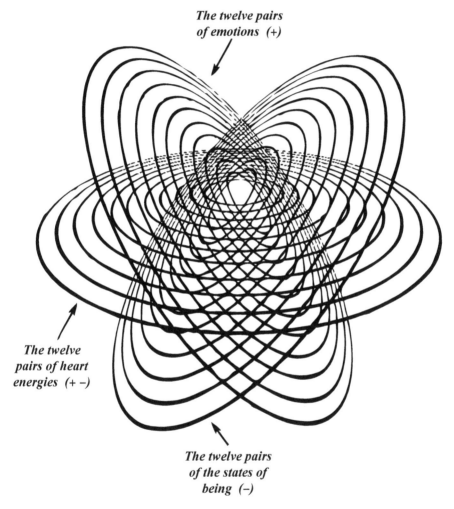

The twelve pairs of emotions (+)

The twelve pairs of heart energies (+ –)

The twelve pairs of the states of being (–)

Originally, the rings each represented a pair that pulsed between their positive and negative aspects. The wheels also pulsed with one another. These were found not only as the grids of the cosmos, but around the body of man.

Following the cosmic changes in December 2008, we no longer pulse between aspects as all fields, light, frequency, etc. are now blended. There are no longer any grids.

The Seven Bodies of Man

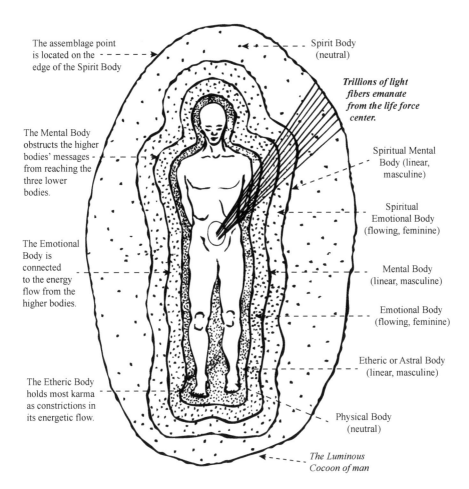

The assemblage point is located on the edge of the Spirit Body

Spirit Body (neutral)

Trillions of light fibers emanate from the life force center.

The Mental Body obstructs the higher bodies' messages from reaching the three lower bodies.

Spiritual Mental Body (linear, masculine)

Spiritual Emotional Body (flowing, feminine)

The Emotional Body is connected to the energy flow from the higher bodies.

Mental Body (linear, masculine)

Emotional Body (flowing, feminine)

Etheric or Astral Body (linear, masculine)

The Etheric Body holds most karma as constrictions in its energetic flow.

Physical Body (neutral)

The Luminous Cocoon of man

The bodies are superimposed over each other and form the luminous cocoon of man. The trillions of light fibers from the life force center penetrate all other bodies forming the spirit body. As a result of the cosmic changes in December 2008, all fields, bodies, light, frequency, etc. are now blended.

Sigils for Grand Master Level Belvaspata

1.
Stu–elavis–klauna   Angel: **Selvi–kluavak-heshpi**

For the removal of any obsolete programming from the light fibers so that the light can be unobstructed in its flow

2.
Ersatvikelesh-uava   Angel: **Kelibap-patrahesbi**

For the clear accessing and interpretation of potential

3.
Kri–ustava-krech-heresbi   Angel: **Stuavu-hespi–echvravi**

For the production of awareness as co-creators of our lives

See the illustration on page 74 for placement of these sigils on the body.

Grand Master Sigils

4.
Brabrat-kluvechspi-anuretvraha   Angel: **Belach-velesh-pavi-stuava-pranut**

For the opening of the capacities for the next level of evolution

5.
Kulbelsta–uvachva-kruneshvavi   Angel: **Gilstra–usbak–vravesh-pi-kla–uva**

For bringing the higher energies into the physical through
pulsing the states of being with the emotions

6.
Kelvikstauvavechspi-straunak Angel: **Barushbelechpa**

For the opening of the door of the pineal to receive awareness, and
the door of the heart to give awareness

Grand Master Sigils

7.

Stuabekbavak-   Angel: **Tristarvamalvashnavek**
klashvisprasteurit

For the flow of information between the higher bodies
and the four lower bodies

8.

Vili–esva-kluchba-stuvechvabi   Angel: **Pritineshva-kulu–esvabi**

For the constant awareness of our highest identity
as our never ending source

9.

Beletrevahupspa–eravi   Angel: **Stuvaver-ehepshpi-**
                                       kluanastrava

For the development of interactive autonomy and sovereignty

The Tenth Sigil in the Tenth Chakra

Connecting the Bodies of Man to the Cosmic Bodies

The Lahun Sigil

Angel Name:
Harahuch-paranech-skava

By using this sigil above the head in the tenth chakra, the Grandmaster connects the person with the cosmic chakra for mutual support.

Placement of the Grand Master Sigils

The cosmos benefits from the healing and the person in
return receives cosmic support.

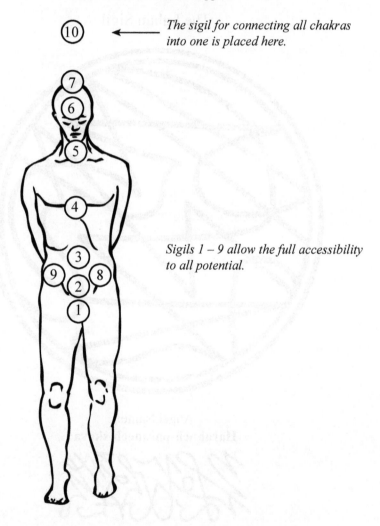

*The sigil for connecting all chakras
into one is placed here.*

*Sigils 1 – 9 allow the full accessibility
to all potential.*

These sigils enable the dissolving of all illusions and heal all
fracturing. They activate the 144 core illuminations of life.

Advanced Sigils for
Master and Grand Master Practitioners

1.
Sigil to Achieve the Optimum Ph
of the Blood *(The alkaline/acidity ratio)*

Kerenech-vravi-hereshvivasta   Angel: **Klubechspi-klanavek**

2.
Sigil for the Fetus of an Unborn Infant

Gershta-uklechva-heresvik   Angel: **Pelevik-ustetvi-hereskla**

3.
Sigil for the Reptilian Brain

Kereshbrikbranavitspaha   Angel: **Kluastragnesvi**

4.
Sigil for the Medulla

Kleshvi-stauherespi   Angel: **Klachvi-meshpi**

Advanced Sigils

5.

Sigils for the Limbic Brain
(helps magnetic/electrical harmony)
Use all of the below for addictions

a.

Kluagna-uvestrava

Angel: **Pereheretruavar**

b.

Perspratnahut-ulu-echblavaa

Angel: **Septiveravaar**

c.

Kluabresbistuvanar

Angel: **Setvikleshvrahaar**

6.

Sigil for the Amygdala

Kersvravigraniksteravi

Angel: **Erekherashvi-krechvi**

Advanced Sigils

7. Sigils for the Neo-Cortex

a.
Birharnavaksetvravish

Angel: **Eravasvetvi**

b.
Granigverevishvahet

Angel: **Gelvishvrasbi**

8. Sigil for the Spinal Cord

Kranighereshnutvavi

Angel: **Kregnish-herespa**

9. Sigil for Cerebrospinal Fluid

Kritvrapeleshvihasvrabi

Angel: **Kru-anegvashpavi**

Advanced Sigils

10.

Sigil for the Pons

Kelstra-hurva-ukluaverespi

Angel: **Ilistrava-klubaberesbi**

11.

Sigil for the Cognitive Heart Center

Kerenastravaa-heshbi

Angel: **Kelstri-uklechvarvaa**

Sigil for the Cognitive Stomach Center
12.
(the 'gut' feeling, or instinct)

Kers-stabaa-hershvi

Angel: **Kluagnetvrich-vravi**

13.
Sigil for the Corpus Callosum
Connecting the Left & Right Brain Hemispheres

Birnik-hevrasta-kregnig

Angel: **Pilnikhershvrata**

Advanced Sigils

14.   Sigil for the Cerebellum

Pelvisprespata-uhurivesbi-kleshvrataa   Angel: **Kliugnesvi-beleshta**

15.   Sigil for the Centrum

Krechvaa-erstu-helesvaa   Angel: **Bilich-hestvik-neshvaa**

16.   Sigil for 12 Cranial Nerves

Kirnit-pleplastavi   Angel: **Hereshvabluavet**

17.   Sigil for Reticular Alarm Activation System
(helpful for hyperactive children)

Kelhasbraseluvitbareshta   Angel: **Pritlaresuit**

Advanced Sigils

18. Sigil for Vagus System

Kelavabra-ushvabi staunag Angel: **Belaviranachtravi**

19. Sigil for the Working Man and Woman
(For freedom from financial bondage and joyous heart-felt work)

Kluha-subatvi-eresta Angel: **Kirinanhursta-plevabi-vechspi**
(male)

Preparing for Initiation
into Belvaspata

Belvaspata: From Initiate to Grand Master Level

Preparations for all Levels of Initiation

Note: *Level I and Level II Initiations may be performed at the same time. Master and Grand Master Initiation may be performed at the same time. This is a result of cosmic changes that occurred in 2008.*

*There still remains a time period of 3-6 months between the combined Level I and Level II initiations **and** the combined Master and Grand Master Initiations.*

Due to the cosmic changes that occurred in December 2008, we no longer have soul groups to accomplish work by proxy, no planetary or cosmic grids and no fields of bodies within our one field. All light, frequency, bodies, fields, etc are combined into the One Being. However, we may now be connected by these individual levels of initiation to that which they represent within the One field.

Level I connects the initiate to the soul group they represent.
Study and internalize the 12 Pairs of Emotions.

A Master or Grand Master of Belvaspata may do initiation for Level I.

Self-initiations may be done with a mentor who is a Master or Grand Master of Belvaspata.

(Level I initiates may use the sigils of Love and others for this level. *See pages 42 and 51.)*

Level II connects the initiate to the planet. Each time a Level II practitioner uses Belvaspata, it affects all of humanity.
Study and internalize the 16 Rays of Light

A Master or Grand Master of Belvaspata may do initiation for Level II.

Self-initiations may be done with a mentor who is a Master or Grand Master of Belvaspata.

(Level II initiates may use the sigils of Love, the sigils of Light and other sigils for this level. *See pages 42, 47 and 51.)*

Master Level removes illusion, connecting the Master to the cosmos in that every time a master practitioner uses Belvaspata, it benefits all of the cosmos.
Study and internalize the 12 Pairs of States of Being.

A Master or Grand Master of Belvaspata may do initiation for Master Level.

Self-initiations may be done with a mentor who is a Master or Grand Master of Belvaspata.

(Master Level initiates may use the sigils of Love, Light, States of Being and some advanced sigils. *See pages 42, 47, 51, 62 and 75.)*

Grand Master Level affects the spiritual emotional, spiritual mental and spirit bodies of all. It is the level to prepare for immortality of the body, as it releases new hormones and opens higher capacities of the endocrine system. It also clears the cosmic pathways and removes old programming of suffering as it connects the initiate with assistance from the highest levels within the cosmos.

Study and internalize the 12 Pairs of Heart Energies.

A Grand Master of Belvaspata may do initiation for Grand Master Level.

Self-initiations may be done with a mentor who is a Grand Master of Belvaspata.

(Grand Master level initiates may use the sigils of all levels of Belvaspata. *See pages 42, 47, 51, 62, 70 and 75.*)

Preparation for Level I

In preparation for Belvaspata's Level I initiation, the initiate must study and internalize the twelve frequencies (emotions) that comprised the twelve frequency bands of the cosmos and have now become a unified field. It may take from a few of hours to an entire day to do this. Once initiated, the practitioner may heal using these frequencies and their sigils.

Before looking at these new frequencies it is important to understand 'what was' so one may more fully appreciate 'what is'.

In the past, there were four basic emotions, each with two opposite poles:

1) Fear (-) / Love (+)
Fear – the desire to retreat
Love – the desire to include within

2) Protectiveness (-) /Anger (+)
Protectiveness – the desire to protect
Anger – the desire to attack/to break up illusion or stuckness

3) Joy (-) / Passion (+)
Joy – the desire to be/to live
Passion – the desire to know

4) Contentment (-) / Pain (+)
Contentment – the desire to keep as is
Pain – the desire to change

These emotions would have pulsed each other from the negative to the positive, from the unknown to the known as we explored portions of the Infinite's Being that had not been fully explored. Often we would find that we over-polarized into one emotion. Then we would attract into our environment the opposite polarity, for example within a relationship, excess anger would need a partner with an over-polarization in protectiveness to provide the balance.

We are now birthing a new paradigm as a result of a major leap in ascension and this has brought about a change in the Laws that govern nature and the cosmos. This has further resulted in a change in emotions. There are now 12 pairs of emotions with some of the old emotions being replaced. No longer do we have pain, fear, protectiveness and anger.

Internalizing The Pure Emotions

To internalize an emotion, we approach it from the largest perspective:

- While in a meditative state, visualize your heart center opening wider and wider until you can imagine seeing the whole Earth in it.
- Imagine and visualize the heart center opening at a rate beyond the speed of light until the solar system, the galaxy and then many galaxies are visible through the heart.
- Continue opening while in deep meditation until the whole cosmos is within you and you have reached the membrane that contains it all.
- You may visualize the large central sun within you and see its arms of light spiraling outwards, consisting of trillions upon trillions of galaxies like specks of light. (You may have another visualization that works for you to achieve maximum expansion — feel free to use it.)
- Remind yourself that you are a consciousness superimposed over all that is and you are all that you see.
- From this large perspective, feel the frequency of one aspect of an Emotional pair ripple through you as you envision all that evokes it. Start with the first Emotion of Love from the pairing of Love and Trust.
- Sustain it until it is strong, potent and all you can feel.
- When you are ready, move on to its 'opposite' or complimentary frequency, Trust.
- As you experience each aspect of an Emotional pair, understand and observe how they complement and inspire one another.

- When you can feel them both, move on to the next Emotional pair while keeping the expanded awareness.
- Each pair of Emotions should be explored and experienced fully. The time necessary for this may be different for each person and for each pair of Emotions being integrated.

While the Pure Emotions are now part of the unified field, it is still important to study and integrate them as they are paired. It is in understanding their specific qualities that we can more fully appreciate how they have combined and yet continue to express their own unique emphasis within the field.

This is the same method that is used to internalize the Rays of Light, the States of Being and the Heart Energies that are given later in this book. As with the Pure Emotions, all are now part of the unified field yet they each maintain their own particular characteristics and essence.

The Twelve Pairs of Emotions

Initially each pair of emotions represented a ring with its masculine and feminine aspects. They pulsed against each other to enhance the qualities of both. The stronger one felt a specific emotion, the deeper one could go into its opposite aspect. In fact, the more strongly an emotion was felt, the more its opposite had to be experienced or an imbalance resulted. For instance, if one did not alternate achievement with fun, it became blind ambition, losing sight of the quality of the journey.

As a result of cosmic changes and the healing of duality and polarity, all emotions form a unified field. Each emotion is a unique expression of the whole and as a pair they inspire one another.

It is essential that the steps be performed in the same order as the frequencies are found within the cosmos, starting from the core emotions of love and trust, and working your way out to growth and satisfaction.

1. Trust and Love

Trust and Love are the core emotions for the new creation of existence and replace fear.

As old programming of fear breaks down in every being, the new reality of trust must reveal itself. It is, after all, what is real; what **is**. All else is just an illusion.

Trusting that our lives are guided in every way by our largest identity that spans all existence, we can release our attempts to control life. But what guides our highest self? The One Life that sustains us all — infinite, timeless and vast.

In your expanded state, feel the essence of the One Infinite Being, the serenity, compassion and ageless wisdom. Feel your expanded being as part of this Infinite's vastness and all-encompassing love. This is what runs all life. Allow yourself to surrender to the guidance and love of the Infinite.

The more we surrender to the One, to ourselves, the deeper our love for all beings grows. We can include them in our love because we see so clearly that the roles we play in our experiences are but small ones on a small stage. When we look further, each being is a unique perspective superimposed over all that is — just as vast as we are and just as deserving of life as a part of the Infinite's Being.

Allow love, trust and total surrender to flood your being until they have become part of all you are.

2. Peace and Inspiration

Peace and Inspiration form the second ring. Peace is the desire to be at home, to feel totally at ease. These rings build on each other; we cannot feel peace when trust is not present, telling us that life is safe. Peace knows that the cosmos is a safe home; that we can relax in the knowledge that we are in the secure hands of our highest self.

The striving that was part of linear progression in the previous cycle, left us feeling we always had to become what we were not. The new creation offers us an unprecedented gift that makes striving unnecessary.

All is available right now in terms of awareness. All we have to do is open the door in each moment using the ascension attitudes.[6] These attitudes come when we cease to strive and are fully at ease within the moment.

This deep peace creates our happiness and acceptance of our body as the center of our cosmic home. This is not something light workers have generally felt. Many have been unaccustomed to dense

---

6 The three ascension attitudes are Praise, Love and Gratitude. For more information read *A Life of Miracles* by Almine.

bodies, having been seeded into humanity as a gift of light for the earth's pivotal role during the cosmic ascension.

They've wanted to leave their bodies, at times even living partially out of body. Where is there to go if we are everywhere at once? We are neither the body nor its experiences. Secure in this knowledge, we can be at peace and enjoy the play.

This feeling of being at peace within ourselves and at home in the cosmos, did not come easily in the previous cycle for another very prominent reason. Since opposites attracted, we were surrounded by opposite energy. The greater our light, the greater the darkness that lurked behind the faces we drew into our environment.

Now that the same energies attract each other, we will be attracting others who live the same high standards of impeccability. We will finally not only feel at home within ourselves but also with others. We must be able to allow those with opposite energies to depart with grace, however, for in keeping with the new laws of the cosmos, their departure is inevitable. It is also inevitable that others with like energies must gravitate towards us.

It is in the deep peace of our being that we access the perfection of all life. It is here inspiration is born. We are now immortal in our individuated beings, and physical immortality is available also through constant states of the ascension attitudes. We have now every reason to be inspired, to build a life of beauty and a legacy that inspires others.

3. Creativity and Pleasure

The link between Creativity and Pleasure is apparent, as the more pleasure fills our life, the more the muse stirs us into creativity; the more creative we become, the more our pleasure increases.

This pair of emotions, together with the previous two rings, forms the core of the new creation. That such pleasant and worthy emotions have replaced anger, pain, fear and protectiveness is a cause for gratitude and great praise. They form the hub, or core of the rings of frequency, inspiring creativity through love — the primary purpose for life.

To be constantly delighted simply takes full awareness of the moment. When we truly experience the wonder of the senses, the beauty of Creation all around us, and the heroism that lies in everyday life, delight will flood our being. Only those unaware, or steeped in thought, can deprive themselves of the pleasure life so freely offers the one who lives in the moment.

4. Acknowledgement and Empathy

See the ever-unfolding perfection underlying appearances. It is not enough to acknowledge that the perfection is there, then feel victimized by someone a while later. Do we truly realize that we have co-created whatever is in our life?

If we do not like what we have created, it is now easier for us to make changes since the very purpose of this new paradigm is creating through love. If we focus on that which we love, new creation will flow. If we focus on that which we do not like, the change will not come. In this new creation, therefore, we have come into our spiritual maturity; we have become co-creators with the Infinite. The perfection is not just there for us to **find**; it is ours to create.

How do we create perfection? We create it by finding it in others, in the moment, in the situation. We create that which we love in another. Light workers no longer need to be surrounded by those of an opposite energy. It should therefore be easy to see perfection in those we draw into our lives.

When we focus on perfection, our ability to find it increases. A light family will increasingly fill our life. In the safety of being among others like us, we empathically connect.

The opposite aspect of acknowledgement is the desire to connect — empathy.

Encounters with those of lower light also allow a heart connection because, in seeing their perfection, we connect with the perfection of their higher selves, not their lowest. In seeing this, we help them to achieve that perfection. But it does not mean we have to allow them into our lives.

Now it is safe for us to connect empathically with others. We are no longer the martyrs. We no longer have to be injured so others may learn. Because our hearts are open, we have become cosmic creators. This is a role so precious and significant that we cannot allow any remaining illusion in another to close off this priceless connection we have with all life — the gift of empathy.

5. Receptivity and Generosity

When a large cycle closes, as has just occurred, not only do opposite poles reverse but, as a consequence, their flow is also reversed. In the previous cycle, light workers were surrounded by those who wanted their light. The takers were not consciously aware of what they were seeking, so they took anything they could get. Light workers, therefore, have been giving for ages while others have been taking.

Now the flow has reversed and the debt has to be paid. There is a law of compensation decreeing that imbalance in any part of existence must have an equal and opposite movement to correct it. This is about to happen as light workers are repaid for all their giving.

There is just one requirement, however, and that is receptivity. After only giving for so long, light workers must break the mindset that can stand in the way of opening to receive. They must, in fact, look forward to it, expect it and envision it.

There has been an agenda associated with others giving to us that has sometimes made us reluctant to receive. But if it is the cosmos settling a score, we are really getting what belongs to us by rights. What does it then matter through what means it chooses to repay us? Let us be filled with receptivity.

When we give, we must not think that such generosity depletes us. Rather let us see how generosity and receptivity form one long continuous flow. Though the wind blowing through the house enters at the window, it leaves through the door. Express both receptivity and generosity joyously.

6. Beauty and Encouragement

It can be said that beauty is just a glimpse into the perfection of the indwelling life behind form. It sees that which has enduring value, like a doorway into eternity. Every time we recognize beauty, we are encouraged (encouragement being its opposite aspect).

Beauty encourages us to create our life as a living work of art. If we see ourselves surrounded by beauty, we are hallowed by it. Moments become meaningful. A hard journey through life becomes not only tolerable, but we feel encouraged enough to believe we can flourish rather than survive.

There are obvious visions of beauty: the sunset over the sea, a child's sleeping face, a new kitten. But the true disciple of beauty doesn't stop there. Encouraged by what has become a treasure hunt for gems of beauty, he seeks to find them in the most unlikely places.

Artists of old saw beauty in the mundane, in another man's trash. They painted the crumbs of a left over meal, the spill of a wineglass. For where others saw only dirty dishes, the artist saw light as it played on crystal and wine and reflected off a wayward spoon.

They did not paint objects, but a dance of light, playfully leading the eye of the observer across the canvas of a captured moment. A famous English watercolorist said at the end of his life that he had never seen anything ugly. These are the words of a true disciple of beauty.

7. Assimilation and Communication

Too little true assimilation of information (which is accessed light) takes place in the world for several reasons:

- True listening to another's words can only take place in the absence of internal dialog. The listener has to stay in the silence of the mind and enter into the other's viewpoint by feeling the communication with the heart.
- The past cycle was left-brain dominated, but the non-verbal communications from the right brain accesses nine times more than did the left brain. Thoughts crowd out the subtle information from the cosmos that is all around us.
- Finding silence is getting more and more difficult. Airplanes roar, car horns blare, appliances hum and then, as though that were not enough, TVs are on whether someone is watching or not. Cell phones make sure that no one has silent time around them. But

it is in silence that we get to know ourselves through listening to our thoughts and desires.

- Conversation and intergenerational communication has dwindled in most cultures where TV has become the substitute for knowing one another.
- We spend too little time in appreciation of nature's wonders, and much of that experience has become action-oriented. All of the natural world and its creatures speak to us through their individual frequencies. We can assimilate their special life song by sitting in silence and feeling it within our cells.

The assimilation of other's communications enriches us. Their diversity can carve new facets in our own life, new perspectives that leave us enhanced. When we feel truly heard, the desire to communicate (its opposite aspect) becomes more active as well.

8. Passion and Joy

When the social conditioning of our lives has left the clear impression that it is unsafe to fully participate in the game of life, we may hang back in the safety of the known, afraid to make ourselves a target by being noticed. We may fear that passion could cause our light to shine so brightly that others might try and tear us down so that their own lack of luster is not as obvious. If we deny our desire to express passionately long enough, we end up being strangers to passion; not knowing how to find it, nor recognize it even if we do. The lateral hypothalamus tells us when we have eaten enough. The ventromedial hypothalamus tells us when we are hungry. In the same way, if we deny the promptings from these portions of the brain, we will end up either obese or anorexic. When that happens we have to gently coach ourselves into recalling how their promptings feel.

When passion beckons, we feel warm and excited; our faces flush and our imagination stirs with questions of "What if?" and "What lies beyond the next horizon?" It inspires us into action and makes us believe we can take risks and build.

We find our passion by following the yearnings our moments of joy evoke within our hearts. It is the lost song the singer feels hiding within the shadows of his mind; the lost rhythm the dancer forever seeks; the mysteries of the cosmos that wait for the scientist or the metaphysician to unlock. It is the desire, inspired by the innocence in our child's eyes, to build a life of wonder and beauty for our family.

If passion has become a stranger to us, we may need to become reacquainted with it one facet at a time. When it is expressed, passion consists of taking risks. It is the precursor to accomplishment and the building of something new. It adds new experiences, further boundaries, and new depth to our lives.

Training ourselves to hear the voice of passion again, we find the yearning of our heart and follow where it leads. We make a concerted effort to break free from the prison bars of ruts and expectations, socially conditioned limitations and self-imposed belief systems that keep us in mediocrity. We take a few minutes a day to dare to dream of what would make our hearts sing. We awake each morning and determine to live the day before us as though it were our last. We look at our lives as though for the first time, with a fresh perspective that can detect the joyless, self-sacrificing areas. With courage and great consideration for the consequences of our actions on others, we implement our first steps to bring the glow of passion back to these areas.

A decision may take a minute to make, but for it to be as life altering as we would want it to be, it must be supported by a firm foundation. This requires planning and a certain amount of analysis. What is the goal? What resources will be needed? Is there a discrepancy between what we need and what we have? How can we fill it? Many businesses fail, taking many dreams with them, because not enough thought was given to what was needed to support them in terms of time and money.

Once a goal is identified, break it into projects and tasks. Many envy the achievements of others, but are not prepared to put in the work. Sometimes it takes burning the candle on both ends to fulfill a dream. It is our passion that keeps our enthusiasm lit and gives us our second wind to fly higher than we ever thought possible.

As passion explores the multitude of possibilities through which we can express, so joy is concentrated on the simplicity of the moment. Joy is a mindset, a certain focus that sees the perfection of the here and now, casting a golden glow over the experiences of yesterday. It turns the mundane into poetry and captures the moment in a still life image.

Milton said: "The mind in its own place and of itself can turn hell into heaven and heaven into hell." Franz Liszt was urged to write his memoirs, but he said: "It is enough to have lived such a life." He found such joy in his experiences; he did not have to externalize them to appreciate them.

Joy can be recognized by the deep feeling of satisfaction it brings, by the feeling that one has come home to oneself. It taps into the quiet place within that nurtures the soul and replenishes the mind. When we are under its spell, joy makes us feel light and young again, connected to the earth and freed from our cares.

Just as building with passion requires careful and disciplined time allocations, living with joy requires us to focus on the details in front of us at the moment. Even if we cannot find even a moment today to do the things we enjoy, we can find the time to enjoy the things we are doing.

In cutting up vegetables to make a stew, we can see the colors of the carrots, explore the different textures of each vegetable and smell the fresh fragrance as we cut through their skins.

Even repetitive work can become a mantra, or a production line a prayer as we send blessings and angelic assistance to the homes where the products will end up. Walking in the crowded street, we can feel the sadness of others but can turn it into joy by envisioning blessings pouring into their lives. The loss in the lives of others can be used to inspire praise and gratitude for the blessings in our own.

In our choice of the joy to fill our leisure time, we look for that which will inspire us into accomplishment. As the joy flows inward on the surface, the passion it inspires folds outward beneath the surface. The greater our joy, the greater the actions it will inspire.

9. Fun and achievement

We have possibly all heard the saying that someone we know 'works hard and plays hard.' That is because the two go hand-in-hand. Fun without achievement is a shallow, unfulfilling life. Achievement without the fun that brings quality to the journey, leads to an equally unsatisfying life. Blind ambition can result from such an imbalance and one becomes blinded as to which achievements would be truly life enhancing.

Fun helps energy flow and prevents us from taking ourselves too seriously. It relieves the tensions we experience during our battles of achievement.

10. Contentment and Enlightenment

Contentment knows that it is living perfect moments; the fire is crackling in the fireplace, a little child with sleep-weighted eyelids is wrapped in a quilt on your lap, while the rain of a winter night beats outside on the window panes.

It is during those moments that we wish everyone on earth could share the feeling of complete contentment. We wish we could enhance the life of a runaway teenager somewhere in a lonely bus station. We want to have the hungry family in the ghetto fed and feeling the inner fulfillment contentment brings.

Such contentment can come as a strong undercurrent of life, rather than as a few fleeting moments. Contentment as a constant companion is the result of deep, meaningful living, of insights gained and inner storms weathered. The desire to enhance and enlighten the life of another is the sincere wish that insight will change despair into contentment for another as well.

11. Empowerment and Humor

Empowerment is the desire to serve. At first, this definition might not make sense. The connection between service and empowerment might seem a bit obscure. The reason is that man has really not understood the proper meaning of service.

Service has often meant assuaging our conscience by giving a handout, not really addressing the deficiency that caused the condition in the first place. True service instead is empowering the individual to find his own way out of the dire straits of his life. This way he has something to show for his hardship: newfound strength or abilities.

The desire to be of service will be never-ending if it is based on need.

It could eventually pull us into the despair of need as well. The balancing factor is humor.

Humor laughs at life, laughs at self and instead of blaming, laughs at the folly of others. It cannot take anything too seriously because it knows without a shadow of doubt that we are just engaged in a play. It helps by empowering the beggar, not because he seems needy, but just because it is his role. The play must go on because it has value.

12. Growth and Satisfaction

Understanding the essence of growth is new. This is because the way growth now takes place is new. It used to be the result of delving (painfully, at times) into the unknown, grappling with its illusion and eventually turning it into the known through experience. When delving into the unknown, fear resulted, often bringing about protectiveness. When the illusion refused to yield its insights, anger tried to break it up.

The emotions associated with growth were not always pleasant and even the word 'growth' often had an unpleasant connotation. Growth is now an expansion that is the result of satisfaction. When we are with those who are energetically incompatible, we experience a shrinking feeling. The new creation brings kindred spirits in the form of family and friends. In the deep satisfaction of their company, we can feel our souls expand.

Growth used to come through opposition. Now it comes through support. How will we know when we have found it? The deep satisfaction of our hearts will tell us we have just lived our highest truth.

Preparation for Level II

The requirement for Level II Initiation is to study and internalize the following sixteen Rays of Light.

The Sixteen Rays of Light

The root of Light is the Infinite, the Goddess Mother of all Creation. She is like the white light that splits into colors. In the new creation into which we have entered, there are sixteen rays of light that move throughout existence. Although our minds may not initially grasp and interpret that we are seeing colors never before seen, we are nevertheless in a new color spectrum. Previously, light reflected the static gridwork of the cosmos; now it reflects cosmic movement.

The Sixteen Rays in a Clockwise Position

1. The Root — During this cycle of existence, Mother/Infinite, the Source of all light, is the root of light. The purity and incorruptible nature of Her Being henceforth safeguards the Cosmic Light against distortion.

As we seek to internalize the root of light in our lives, let us be always mindful that we exist in the holiness of Her Being and that we can dedicate every action, every breath we take in love, praise and gratitude to the One Being that sustains us and gives us life.

In meditation, let us see ourselves become as vast as the cosmos and as we linger there, let us know we have become one with the Infinite Mother, that in such expanded awareness, we are being cradled in Her loving arms. It is here where we will find the Source of all light.

2. Faith — The nature of faith has changed for this creation. Formerly, it was a mindset that re-created itself. In other words, the most prevalent and dominant thoughts ended up creating our environment. Because our thoughts were generally chaotic, we created chaotic conditions on Earth.

The new creations do not come through thought, but through the heart. We create through love, praise and gratitude — a way that prevents us from creating more chaos. Faith, as a way to create our reality, has to therefore reflect this change. The new way to understand faith would be as the conscious creation of reality through an attitude of love. Envision how you would like to live life, and flood the images with love, praise and gratitude that such joyous manifestations can be yours.

3. Balance — The light-ray of balance represents the essence of what the Mayans call 'Movement and Measure.' Balance is not static, but rather consists of the dynamic movement between expanding boundaries. In other words, it moves between positive and negative aspects within existence, always pulling them slightly further apart.

As an example, a balanced life pulses between beingness and doingness. The deeper we enter into the peace of our being, the more we can accomplish with our actions (our 'doingness'). In this way, both our passive and pro-active aspects are strengthened and enhanced. In these deepening pulsations lie the expansion and growth of the being.

4. Abundance — The true meaning of abundance has been colored by the beautiful and uplifting purpose of our new existence, creation through the heart. Before, we hoped that life would deliver abundance. Now we are limited only by how large we can dream and how much love we can pour into our dreams and visions.

While doing this, we continue to broadcast heartfelt gratitude throughout the cosmos for what we have. Increases do not occur where there is an absence of gratitude for present gifts. Conversely, whatever we are grateful for increases.

Generosity also increases supply. If we truly understand that we are co-creators of our realities, then our supply has no limit. In giving, we simply open the sluices of manifestation a little wider. If we have love, praise and gratitude, we open it wider still; clustering awareness into manifesting our created realities.

5. Wisdom — It has been said that wisdom is applied knowledge. Previously, we had to interpret principles that lay hidden within the illusion of the former cycle of existence. Now all illusion has been solved and the new creation lies before us like a pristine uncharted land. What knowledge is there to apply?

The knowledge that needs to be interpreted through our lives is the knowledge of the self we see mirrored within those of like energy. In them, we see ourselves and learn about what we are. Learning by observing those energies in others, we become more of what we are and find new ways of applying them in our lives.

6. Mercy — Mercy no longer means tolerating the dysfunctional in our midst. In fact, the opposite is true. Because opposite light and frequency (emotion) now attract, the most merciful way of living is to surround ourselves with authentic, love-filled people who make our hearts sing. As we feel joy, it is automatically drawn to its opposite aspect, the most joyless places in the cosmos.

Mercy therefore resembles a form of 'tough love,' a refusal to indulge the clinging to old patterns of illusion as some will want to do. The repelling of those of opposite energies used to be considered 'uncharitable' — now not living our highest truth is.

7. Diversity — The greatest period of growth for any group of beings is when there is unity within diversity, creating interdependency. The slowest growth, and ultimately stagnation, occurs when there is uniformity. We see this in tribal life. The dynamic within the group is one of dependency, keeping its members in an infantile state.

Because the new creation stresses 'sameness,' diversity within the 'sameness' is absolutely vital. If this were not the case, the possibility of over-polarization into the known (accessed light) would be a very real concern. The inevitable result of such over-polarization is stagnation. Although we are to study the beautiful qualities of others, we are in fact studying our own.

We can only recognize that which we have within — the major reason why light-promoters have been so easily deceived by those of ill intent. Although what we see is what we are, every other person is like a uniquely colored lens through which his beam of light shines. When this diversity is observed and appreciated, it brings richness to our lives.

8. Energy — The deep secret behind this fact is that matter and energy have merged. This has already occurred. The gods and goddesses in human form have become 100% energy and are moving into becoming an even more refined form of light. A whole new reality is being born, one in which the Mother Goddess Herself will reign on this most pivotal planet, Earth.

9. Bliss — Bliss is a result of a vast expansive perception that effects the vibration of a body's cells. It is a state of profound praise, love and gratitude generated by an eternal perspective.

The gift of bliss is that old patterns melt away in its presence; constrictions in the flow of energy release. Others experience healings and growth by grace. In a new creation where we are able to access awareness by grace through the ascension attitudes, bliss is more readily present. As one of the rays of light, it offers growth through grace and births hope that anyone can achieve the pinnacle of enlightenment through love, praise and gratitude.

10. Perception — Perception used to come through the gifts of challenge and hardship. Through the friction of life's experiences turning the unknown into the known, perception exacted a high cost.

In the cycle of existence just completed, perception yielded emotion as the primary way of promoting change. Perception birthed the realities of our lives. In this creation, our emotions primarily steer our course, affecting our perception. The more profound our emotions, the more they birth our hopes and dreams into reality.

Imagine our lives as a sphere of existence filled with twelve concentric circular frequency bands (emotion). If the emotions strengthen, the bands expand. Light rays bounce through these bands. If they expand, the light rays have to move through a larger sphere; therefore they have to move faster to complete their pattern. The more intense the emotion, the faster we get our perception.

11. Presence — The Mother of All has a specific 'flavor' to Her light — a personality that expresses Her Being in this cycle of Creation more than any other. Within this ray of light, the presence of the Infinite Divine Being is accessed and known.

The stillness of Mother's ancient moments, timeless and eternal, the tempestuousness of her cataclysmic change, all can be felt through this ray. The reflections of the facets of Her Being are expressed in the stupendous variety and exquisite beauty of Her creations. We can study the Mother's Being by seeing Her face in the reflections of the cosmos.

The study and interpretation of the majesty and glory of the Infinite Mother is really the study of self. We are Her facets, Her reflections. We can only recognize in Her what we are in ourselves. This creation is dedicated to studying the known, that which we are, by accessing it within the divine presence of the Mother of Creation.

12. Hope — Hope is a state of mind that lives with eyes and heart firmly fixed on the most beneficial outcome. Hope has taken on an entirely new meaning since our reason for being has become the creation of that which we love through the heart.

Hope is the vision we hold as we fan the flame of its creation through love, praise and gratitude. This acts upon the substance of things hoped for, formed from tiny fragments of awareness that have always existed, but have now become abundantly available for us to create with.

An attitude is comprised of both love and light. The attitudes of ascension are really the positively charged aspects of awareness. The awareness particles comprise the opposite (negative) aspect.

Awareness also consists of both love (frequency) and light (where opposites attract). The little rays rush towards the source of the ascension attitudes. Here they roll, cluster and fill the mold created by hope.

13. Mastery — Mastery advocates a life lived from complete authenticity, self-discipline, and inner balance. Mastery is a combination of many attributes that take dedication and focus to achieve. Previously these attributes took years to cultivate, one painstaking step at a time.

With awareness immediately available and with time's collapse into the moment, mastery is now at our fingertips. It takes a mindset that always acts from our highest vision, remembering that we are a vast being superimposed over all that is and that wherever we are is the center of our cosmos.

Mastery acts with the utmost impeccability and sensitivity in realizing that every action, every thought, impacts the whole. With such awareness, each act becomes an act of love for the interconnectedness of all life.

14. Discovery — The great significance of the introduction of this ray of light into Creation is as follows:

• The previous cycles of creation were descension cycles, containing a great deal of distorted light. The descension was due to self-centered and separative patriarchal rule. This distorted emotion created fear, anger, pain and protectiveness. Thus we were driven further and further down into density.

• It did not have to be this way. Mother had given freedom of choice to Her creations. The choices of Mother's creations brought about these painful descension cycles and ultimate rebellion and destruction.

• The way it was meant to be was through joyful discovery of the unknown, much the same way the ancient mariners set forth to explore the uncharted seas. It was supposed to be a treasure hunt — finding the gems within our being lying in the dust of the unknown. Through many of the choices made by the higher gods, the adventure of discovery became a nightmare. The reinstallation of this precious ray of light is a wonderful gift as we study the known.

15. Power — In the new creation, all of the previous rays of light moved into the ray of Power, which then moved to birth the 16th ray, as follows:

- All previous rays moved into the one ray, namely the ray of Power.
- The one ray of Power then moved into the inner emotional sphere of trust/love with the brilliance of all fifteen rays.
- The great power and light caused the emotional sphere to spin counterclockwise.
- The rapid spinning shot out all fifteen previous rays plus an additional one, a pink ray embodying absolute truth.

The first fifteen rays previously mentioned had originally been meant to become available as the cosmos ascended. This would have provided the cosmos with the ability to move on to a new existence beyond (as we have just done) without having to go through numerous and repetitive cycles of ascension and decension. Due to the distortion chosen by some of the lords of the light rays at the very pinnacle of existence, the Mother of Creation never gave additional rays until now.

16. Truth — This newly born ray of truth is a new form of this principle. Truth was previously that which was sought without, through the phantoms of illusion clustered about us, attracted to our light. Truth is no longer found without — after all, we are in a play that has yet to be written. There are no preconceived guidelines here. It lies before us, pristine as this newborn ray of truth. This ray is the firstborn child of the cosmos; it is to be felt in our hearts as *The Ring of Truth*.

Preparation for Master Level

The requirement for Master Level initiation is to study and internalize the States of Being.

While they are now part of the unified field, it is still important to understand the individual qualities and how they combine to fully appreciate the unique emphasis that each contributes.

The Twelve Pairs of States of Being

1. Praise (+) As a state of being it is slightly different than when it is an attitude. Attitudes have more perception. Praise is the surge of deep, exultant feeling that comes from accessing the highest aspect within. It is the triumph of recognizing the perfection underlying appearances.

Glory (-) Glory is the maintenance of the highest aspect of ourselves as a being as vast as the cosmos, and its expression in our lives. In other words, it is when we live life from our largest perspective.

2. Exploration (+) Exploration is the pushing beyond previous boundaries of expression so that new creation and deeper expression can take place for the sake of growth.

Harmony (-) Harmony is the state of being that results from being in step with the blueprint or will of the Infinite; when smaller segments of Creation express synchronistically with the largest purpose of life.

3. Gratitude (+) This state of being results from encountering the true nature of the cosmos as one that supports all life, the recognition of the nurturing of the Divine in our lives.
Guidance (-) The revelation of the most life-enhancing choices along our path and the uncovering of the blueprint of our existence. (**Note:** Within the irrevocable overall purpose of our lives there are now more choices and freedom of expression available than ever as we enter our spiritual maturity.)

4. Discernment (+) Although all unknown portions of Mother's Being have been solved during the cycles of the Fall, there is nevertheless always a mystery as to which expression of the known portions of Her Being would be most life-enhancing. The discernment comes when our hearts reveal this mystery.
Transparency (-) Transparency is the revelation of a portion of existence that reflects the purity of absolute truth.

5. Understanding (+) When we regard our true identity as a being as vast as the cosmos, all is **within** our consciousness that is **without** our bodies. Understanding comes when the light fibers within our bodies light up, or come on line, as a result of something outside our bodies revealing its information.
Reflection (-) When something is encountered in life that evokes an emotional response, it is worthy of study and further scrutiny. It is an indicator of whether we have lived our highest truth. It may also be an indicator of a mystery waiting to reveal itself. Reflection will show whether what we have understood is worthy of implementing and incorporating into our life.

6. Embrace (+) Embrace is the reaching to incorporate more of the vastness of existence into our compassionate understanding and acceptance.

Ecstasy (-) Ecstasy results from the inclusiveness of our vision that sees each life as its own.

7. Manifestation (+) Fifty percent[7] of life is ours to manifest and create at will; that part of life in which we can creatively contribute to the big picture. Manifestation occurs when awareness clusters itself into the circumstances of our lives, pulled forth by the emotions of our hearts as well as our attitudes.

Inevitability (-) Each of us plays a part in contributing to the growth and evolution of the large plan or pattern of life. This constitutes inevitability: the experiences we are required to live according to our mutual contract with the Infinite. Because growth comes through mutual support, the large plan also writes in some 'key moments' — moments of support that are given in our own lives depending on which choices we make. This is part of the set circumstances, of inevitability, in our lives.

8. Oneness (+) Living the deep awareness that all beings are part of us makes us aware of the interconnectedness of life. We gain this understanding by opening ourselves to include all parts of existence.

Contentment (-) Contentment results when oneness occurs and life flows through us without obstruction. We feel that we have come home.

---

7 As of May 2007.

9. Integration (+) The praiseworthy parts of life beckon for us to make them our own — to integrate them as a part of us. That which we find unworthy of integrating, nevertheless has gifts in the form of insights that are worth making our own and should not be dismissed.

Evolution (-) As the caterpillar grows with each bite of the leaf it eats, so we grow in depth of wisdom and perception with each part of our experiential learning that we make our own and integrate. Change for the better is therefore the one constant in a life well lived.

10. Play (+) The spontaneous and lighthearted interaction with the unexpected creates a useful flexibility. It spontaneously and abundantly creates a grace and ease of interaction with life in the moment.

Flexibility (-) The cumbersome weight of self-reflection, self-pity and self-importance weighs down the journey and keeps us locked into points of view. Any viewpoint could, in the next moment, be obsolete as life changes constantly, thought by thought.

11. Perception (+) Much abuse of power has occurred by reversing the polarity of power and perception. Power is the state of being that results from perception, not the other way around. It is perception that must actively be sought in our world, not power.

Power (-) Power as a feminine pole is vastly more powerful than power that is masculine and separative. Power that is feminine, and therefore inclusive in nature, is the power that is aligned with all that is.

12. Retention (+) To retain or allow something to flow through our lives requires our making a simple choice. The only real question in all existence is what is life-enhancing and what is not. That which is, we retain as our own.

Conductivity (-) Conductivity when fully lived brings our lives into a state of grace. The alternative, resistance to that which we choose not to retain, leaks energy and lowers consciousness. It embodies the complete surrender to life.

Preparation for Grand Master Level

The requirement for Grand Master Level Initiation is to study and internalize the Twelve Heart Energies of the Zhong-galabruk

The Heart Energies from the Zhong-Galabruk

Heart energies were born when the Pure Emotions and the States of Being pulsed each other. The feminine aspect of one (either a Pure Emotion or a State of Being) pulsed with the masculine aspect of the other. This interaction produced particles of awareness that had a negative polarity in relation to the already existing awareness particles spread throughout the cosmos. The deeper or stronger one aspect pulsed, the deeper the other responded and the stronger the quality of heart energy that was born.

As the Heart Energies were produced, the Heart Energies themselves 'pulsed' to form an enhanced and balanced Heart Energy. The healing of polarity and duality has meant that they are all now part of a unified field and as such, each is a unique emphasis within that field.

Awareness used to move until August of 2006 when massive changes occurred to the structure and nature of existence. Now awareness only moves in response to love, praise and gratitude as a magnetizing force.

But the awareness particles emitted by the heart will vary from person to person, determined by his or her heart energies. When there is an emission of these negative particles of awareness, they hover in that person's environment until directed to create through love, praise and gratitude focused on a specific set of circumstances. As the cloud of awareness particles surrounds the person, these particles (although not moving directionally) vibrate. The dance, or vibration, of the particles is very much affected by the energetic qualities of the heart. When these particles dance in a similar way to someone else's, we can deduce that their heart energies are the same and that, since same energies attract, there will be a strong attraction.

Note: In August 2006, it was written by Mother in the Book of Life (which determines the laws of the cosmos), that heart energy will always be the determining factor (in other words stronger), rather than light or frequency in any relationship. In that way, light workers will be attracted to one another, rather than have their similar light and frequencies repelling each other (remember: same light and frequency repel, same energies attract — the principles behind the effectiveness of Belvaspata as a healing method).

The Creation of the Heart Energies

Emotions	*and*	States of Being	*give*	Heart Energies
Love (+)		Glory (-)		Ecstasy (+)
Trust (-)		Praise (+)		Embrace (-)
Inspiration (+)		Harmony (-)		Insight (+)
Peace (-)		Exploration (+)		Appreciation (-)
Creativity (+)		Guidance (-)		Inspiration (+)
Pleasure (-)		Gratitude (+)		Love (-)
Empathy (+)		Transparency (-)		Truth (+)
Acknowledgement (-)		Discernment (+)		Clarity (-)
Generosity (+)		Reflection (-)		Manifestation (+)
Receptivity (-)		Understanding (+)		Gratitude (-)
Encouragement (+)		Ecstasy (-)		Rejoicing (+)
Beauty (-)		Embrace (+)		Praise (-)
Communication (+)		Inevitability (-)		Harmony (+)
Assimilation (-)		Manifestation (+)		Wisdom (-)
Passion (+)		Contentment (-)		Fulfillment (+)
Joy (-)		Oneness (+)		Presence (-)
Achievement (+)		Evolution (-)		Growth (+)
Fun (-)		Integration (+)		Balance (-)
Enlightenment (+)		Flexibility (-)		Evolution (+)
Contentment (-)		Play (+)		Surrender (-)
Empowerment (+)		Power (-)		Discovery (+)
Humor (-)		Perception (+)		Awareness (-)
Growth (+)		Conductivity (-)		Acceptance (+)
Satisfaction (-)		Retention (+)		Allowing (-)

The Heart Energies

1. Ecstasy (+)   +   Embrace (-)   =   Divine Compassion
2. Insight (+)   +   Appreciation (-)   =   Reverence
3. Inspiration (+)   +   Love (-)   =   Pure Creativity
4. Truth (+)   +   Clarity (-)   =   Absolute truth
5. Manifestation (+)   +   Gratitude (-)   =   Impeccability
6. Rejoicing (+)   +   Praise (-)   =   Celebration
7. Harmony (+)   +   Wisdom (-)   =   Timing
8. Fulfillment (+)   +   Presence (-)   =   Focus
9. Growth (+)   +   Balance (-)   =   Strength
10. Evolution (+)   +   Surrender (-)   =   Grace
11. Discovery (+)   +   Awareness (-)   =   Clarity
12 Acceptance (+)   +   Allowing (-)   =   Harmlessness

The Heart Energies

1. Ecstasy (+) + Embrace (-) = Divine Compassion

Ecstasy as a positive factor is active: it is the broadcasting, or reaching out, of the ecstatic song of the heart. Wherever it reaches, the heart embraces; the heart includes in its compassionate embrace. Divine compassion can therefore be described as the ecstatic embrace of the heart.

2. Insight (+) + Appreciation (-) = Reverence

Insight, as a positive aspect, probes behind the illusion of appearances, finding the perfection underlying all life. True illusion, as unsolved portions of existence, no longer exist. All has been solved. But the 'illusion' of taking things at face value continues. Insight refuses to take life at face value, finding the divine within. The response of the heart to seeing the divine order behind illusion is one of honoring and appreciation of life. From this vantage point, life is lived with reverence for all life, refining the person living this way and hallowing his experience.

3. Inspiration (+) + Love (-) = Pure Creativity

Inspiration is a positive quality, actively seeking out that which uplifts and inspires in what it observes. What uplifts and presents us with inspiration evokes a deep love in our hearts. It creates a desire for us to be in its presence. The combination of the inspiration plus the love we feel for that which inspires, brings forth the desire to create through the heart — the place of pure creation.

4.Truth (+) + Clarity (-) = Absolute truth

When truth, as we see it, is lived at its highest level, we start to express and live from a situation of clarity; where we are true, not only to others, but to ourselves. In clarity and truth we become aware of our motives' origins. (Toltec mystics call it stalking ourselves.) As we eliminate fear, protectiveness, anger and pain as motives, the reasons for taking action or making choices become clear and guide the promptings of our heart. The pure guidance of our heart comes from the blueprint of the Infinite (that which the Mother Goddess is), which is absolute truth.

5. Manifestation (+) + Gratitude (-) = Impeccability

The loss of impeccability is the result of failing to see the support of the greater scheme of our lives; of not recognizing that we are not alone. It is in thinking that we have to fend for ourselves that we act in a way that does not enhance the interconnectedness of life. In allowing life's perfection to manifest in our lives in whatever way it wants to, and knowing with gratitude that we are sustained at all times, impeccability is born.

6. Rejoicing (+) + Praise (-) = Celebration

Rejoicing is a choice. It chooses to find that which is praiseworthy over that which is not. If one looks for that which is flawed, it is easy to find. Looking for that which one can rejoice in might take more work. In doing so, our life changes day by day into a song of praise, and transforms itself into one of celebration.

7. Harmony (+) + Wisdom (-) = Timing

There is a flow to life — subtle currents that determine the course of events. There is a time to act and a time to reflect; a time for output and a time for input. Our lives unfold with grace and in perfect timing when we have wisdom to stay in harmony with the soft whisperings of destiny. To have the wisdom to obey these inner whisperings, takes restraint. To hear them takes the silence of the mind of one who has ceased to oppose life.

8. Fulfillment (+) + Presence (-) = Focus

Toltec seers have given the sage advice to use death as an advisor; to live each moment as though it were our last, with the focus it deserves. The moment is the pivot point upon which all of life pivots. It is therefore that which holds life's potential. As such, it deserves our full presence so that it can yield its full potential. In other words, the moment can fulfill its promises of a new tomorrow, unfettered by yesterday's expectations. If tomorrow comes from the moment, but the moment is not lived in a fulfilling manner, with presence and focus, where will the future come from? It will instead be formed by our yesterdays, haphazardly and as a repeat of what went before.

9. Growth (+) + Balance (-) = Strength

Growth that is unsupported lacks strength. Growth is always tested, for gained knowledge has to become experiential knowledge to be truly useful. Without balance to bolster it, it will lack the strength to pass the testing of experience. Growth internally produces external change. If change is not balanced with rest, or our coming home to ourselves (more detailed information on "Wings and Roots" by Almine, available as an MP3), we will have wings but no roots. It is the dynamic pulsing between wings and roots that gives us our strength.

10. Evolution (+) + Surrender (-) = Grace

Grace is the enviable result of the ability to live life with full cooperation. The surrender and trust of allowing life to evolve at its own pace, and in its own way, brings to our lives the grace of Mastery. It does not only require that we allow life to flow through us, but that we learn from it as it does, evolving through the insights it bestows.

11. Discovery (+) + Awareness (-) = Clarity

We have examined clarity in Heart Energy number four as the complete honesty with ourselves that requires a transparency of our motives. Clarity as an end result can be described as the certainty of what our next step is. The journey of existence becomes a journey of discovery when lived with the utmost awareness; an awareness born of the humility to know that only a fool can assume to know what the next moments will be. A life of clarity is not outcome oriented. It only knows that through living in the fullest awareness, the discovery of the next step will be achieved by living this one well, and thus a journey of clarity unfolds one step at a time.

12. Acceptance (+) + Allowing (-) = Harmlessness

Injury to life comes when we step out of contracts: when we fight and resist life's circumstances, keeping others and ourselves from growing. We often want life to change, but refuse to accept that we have to change ourselves. It is when we accept the moment for what it is, but allow change to come where it is needed by changing ourselves, that we fulfill life's contracts. Only then does life become empowered, rather than one of victimhood. When we feel life is out of control, we try to control its unfolding, causing harm to the interconnected web of life. By accepting our part of directing the play, but also allowing the script to unfold, life is lived harmlessly.

Integrating the Heart Energies

The 12 Pairs of Heart Energies are studied and internalized in the same way as the 12 Pairs of Emotions, the 16 Rays of Light and the States of Being have been. While they are now part of the unified field, it is still important to understand the individual qualities and how they combine to fully appreciate the unique emphasis that each contributes.

1) While in a meditative state, visualize your heart center opening wider and wider until you can imagine seeing the whole Earth in it.

2) Imagine and visualize the heart center opening at a rate beyond the speed of light until the solar system, the galaxy and then many galaxies are visible through the heart.

3) Continue opening while in deep meditation until the whole cosmos is within you and you have reached the membrane that contains it all.

4) You may visualize the large central sun within you and see its arms of light spiraling outwards, consisting of trillions upon trillions of galaxies like specks of light.

5) Remind yourself that you are a consciousness superimposed over all that is and you are all that you see.

6) From this large perspective, feel the frequency and the quality of one aspect of a Heart Energy pairing rippling through you. Start with the first Heart Energy of Ecstasy from the pairing of Ecstasy and Embrace.

7) Sustain it until it is strong, potent and all you can feel.

8) Then when you are ready move onto its complimentary aspect, Embrace.

9) As you experience the Heart Energy pairing, understand and observe how they complement and inspire one another to form an enhanced and balanced Heart Energy. For example observe and feel how the pairing of Ecstasy and Embrace combine to form Divine Compassion

10) When you are ready, move on to the next set of Heart Energies while maintaining expanded awareness.

11) Repeat steps 6 – 9 above for the remaining Heart Energies.

12) Each set of Heart Energies should be explored and experienced fully. The time necessary for this may be different for each person and for each pair being integrated.

Initiations:
Initiating another into Belvaspata

Belvaspata Initiations by a Master

Note: A Master Practitioner of Belvaspata can initiate up to Master Level of Belvaspata. A Grand Master Practitioner of Belvaspata can initiate all levels of Belvaspata.

Opening and Closing Initiations: Level I Initiation sigils are used for Level I initiations and to open all other initiations, in order to increase receptivity. The love, praise and gratitude sigils are always used for closing an initiation to seal the frequencies of the sigils within the body. (See Example Level II Initiation Sigil on page 131.)

When using the sigils for Initiations:

Step 1. Follow the directions as indicated on the sigils themselves for each level.

Step 2. Draw the sigil **3 times** over the area indicated — for this sigil it is the lower abdomen.

Step 3. Call (say) the quality of the sigil either out loud or silently **3 times** in Mother's language: **Kel-a-visva-uravech.**

Step 4. State the following: "By the power of this Sigil which I hold in my hand, I call in the Angel (insert angel name)" and call (say) the angel name either out loud or silently **3 times** in Mother's language, asking the angel to place the sigil in the desired location.

Look at the angel sigil while calling the angel name: Krunechva-atruha. (It is not necessary to draw the sigil for the angel name.)

Step 5. Complete all initiations by making a closing statement that declares the new level of mastery achieved by the initiate. As an example, you may use the following statement or something similar:

"By the power vested in me, I declare that (insert name of initiate) is now a (insert initiation level) of Belvaspata, Healing of the Heart. We give thanks to our teacher, Almine and to the Infinite for the sacred gift of Belvaspata."

Step 6. Close all initiations by drawing the sigils for love, praise and gratitude. You may draw them above the heart or over the entire body. (See Closing Sigils to end a Session on page 138.)

Example of Level II Initiation Sigil

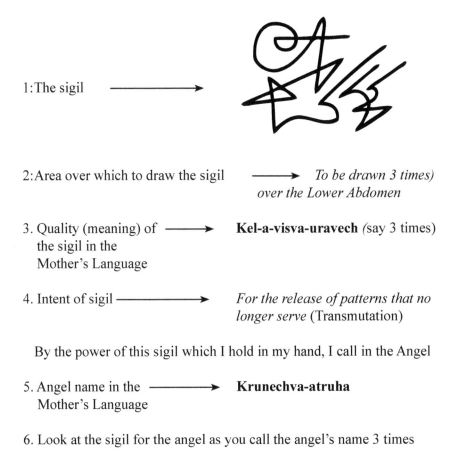

1: The sigil

2: Area over which to draw the sigil ⟶ *To be drawn 3 times) over the Lower Abdomen*

3. Quality (meaning) of ⟶ **Kel-a-visva-uravech** *(*say 3 times)
the sigil in the
Mother's Language

4. Intent of sigil ⟶ *For the release of patterns that no longer serve* (Transmutation)

By the power of this sigil which I hold in my hand, I call in the Angel

5. Angel name in the ⟶ **Krunechva-atruha**
Mother's Language

6. Look at the sigil for the angel as you call the angel's name 3 times

Angel Sigil

Level I Initiation Sigils

All 3 Level I sigils are used at the start of all healing sessions and prior to initiation into other levels of Belvaspata.

1.

Bla-utva-pata (say 3 times)
For the Opening of the Mind

To be drawn 3 times over the forehead

By the power of this sigil that I hold in my hand, I call in the angel **Rutsetvi-uru-bach** (say three times and look at the angel sigil) to place this sigil within the forehead.

Angel Sigil:

2.

Kru-vech-pa-uru-rek (say 3 times)
For the Opening of the Heart

To be drawn 3 times over the heart

By the power of this sigil that I hold in my hand, I call in the angel **Iornumubach** (say three times and look at the angel sigil) to place this sigil within the heart.

Angel Sigil:

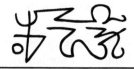

3.

Kel-a-vis-ba-vah (say 3 times)
For the Opening of the Body

To be drawn 3 times over the navel

By the power of this sigil that I hold in my hand, I call in the angel **Tru-ararir-pleva** (say three times and look at the angel sigil) to place this sigil within the navel.

Angel Sigil:

Level II Initiation Sigils

(When healing, Level II initiation sigils may be used in conjunction with Level I's sigils to start the session.)

1.

Kel-a-visva-uravech (say 3 times)
For the release of patterns that no longer serve (transformation)

To be drawn 3 times over the Lower Abdomen

By the power of this sigil that I hold in my hand, I call in the angel **Krunechva-atruha** (say three times and look at the angel sigil) to place this sigil within the lower abdomen.

Angel Sigil:

2.

Trech-su-ba-reshvi (say 3 times)
For transmuting matter to higher light

To be drawn 3 times over the Solar Plexus

By the power of this sigil that I hold in my hand, I call in the angel **Mirakluvael** (say three times and look at the angel sigil) to place this sigil within the solar plexus.

Angel Sigil:

3.

Pata-uru-hut-vi (say 3 times)
For transfiguring illusion to light

To be drawn 3 times over the Sternum

By the power of this sigil that I hold in my hand, I call in the angel **Kelevi-traunar** (say three times and look at the angel sigil) to place this sigil within the sternum.

Angel Sigil:

Level II Initiation Sigils

4.

Kers-baur-veshpi (say 3 times)
For sanctification

To be drawn 3 times over the Crown

By the power of this sigil that I hold in my
hand, I call in the angel **Trechbar-uru-heresvi**
(say three times and look at the angel sigil) to
place this sigil within the crown.

Angel Sigil:

5.

Klet-sut-manarech (say 3 times)
For attracting light into the voice

To be drawn 3 times over the Throat

By the power of this sigil that I hold in my
hand, I call in the angel **Viliveshbi-keres-na**
(say three times and look at the angel sigil) to
place this sigil within the throat.

Angel Sigil:

6.

Vis-beles-pah-rech-vi (say 3 times)
For attracting healing frequencies into the
hands

To be drawn 3 times over each hand

By the power of this sigil that I hold in my
hand, I call in the angel **Kru-echna-vilshpreva**
(say three times and look at the angel sigil) to
place this sigil within each hand.

Angel Sigil:

Level II Initiation Sigils

7.

Nen-hersh-bi-klet-rasut (say 3 times)
For DNA activation of the codes of light

To be drawn 3 times over the Root Chakra

By the power of this sigil that I hold in my hand, I call in the angel **Ku-ulu-vet** (say three times and look at the angel sigil) to place this sigil within the root chakra.

Angel Sigil:

8.

Vele-echs-bi-kluatret (say 3 times)
For creating movement in light

To be drawn 3 times over the Alpha Chakra (1 hand length below the base of the spine)

By the power of this sigil that I hold in my hand, I call in the angel **Belech-his-pavatra** (say three times and look at the angel sigil) to place this sigil within the alpha chakra.

Angel Sigil:

*Also call in the angel **Kelipretvaha** to place this sigil into the Earth.*

9.

Nun-mer-stararot-belch-spi (say 3 times)
For bringing in the new template of frequency

To be drawn 3 times over the bottom of each foot

By the power of this sigil that I hold in my hand, I call in the angel **Kretna-ulu-vesbi** (say three times and look at the angel sigil) to place this sigil within the bottom of each foot.

Angel Sigil:

Master Level Initiation Sigil

This sigil is **NOT** to be used on clients. It is only to be used for initiation.

Belveresnukvi

All Becomes One

The sigil is drawn 3 times over each of the following areas in the order given:

1. bottom of each foot
2. alpha chakra
3. root chakra
4. lower abdomen
5. navel
6. solar plexus
7. heart
8. sternum
9. throat
10. forehead
11. crown
12. palms of both hands
13. 10" above crown

After drawing the sigil 3 times in each location, say the following:
Bel-veres-nuk-vi, Bel-veres-nuk-vi, Bel-veres-nuk-vi, All Becomes One

By the power of this angel sigil that I hold in my hand,
I call in the angel **Urhetvi**. (say the angel name 3 times as you
look at the angel sigil) to place the Master Sigil in each of the
following locations of the body. (Read the list above from 1 – 13)

Angel Sigil:

Grand Master Level Initiation Sigil

This sigil is **NOT** to be used on clients. It is only to be used for initiation.

Kluagvanesvi-elu-achvraheresh-vi-slaulag
(say three times)

To be drawn 3 times over the heart

By the power of the angel sigils that I hold in my hand, I call
in the following angels who support this initiatory level:
(say each angel name three times while looking at the angel sigil)

Brua–kranuvig–stela–u–achvraba

Kersh–heruvit–pele–ach–uvespi–klauna

Stuapruanatvi–keleshna

Closing Sigils for a Session or Initiation

Praise

Love

Gratitude

PART VII

Self-Initiation into Belvaspata

Guidelines for Self-Initiation

Self-initiation means that you initiate yourself into Belvaspata, however, it is required that you work with a mentor who is a Master or Grand Master in order for your initiation to be considered valid. Another person cannot do this for you either long-distance or over the phone.

In the case of self-initiation, completion of the preparation work (as listed below) increases the frequency of the initiate so they are prepared to receive the initiation. This is accomplished for each specific level by:

- Completing the preparation for each level of initiation — as in the internalizing of the specific Emotions, Rays of Light, States of Being or Heart Energies. The preparation for each level is the same for both self-initiation as for initiation by a Master or Grand Master.
- Translation of the Infinite Mother's language for the level of initiation using the Mother's alphabet.
- Drawing the appropriate sigils for the level of Initiation.
- Completing the ceremony of self-initiation by asking the angels to place the sigils in your body and speaking the initiation in the language of the Infinite. It is important that you speak the words yourself.

The time frame between initiations remains the same. Level I and Level II may be done at the same time, as may Master and Grand Master Levels. There still must however be at least 3 months between Level I and Level II **and** Master and Grand Master Levels. Be guided by what is right for you. Regular use of the sigils is an important aspect of Belvaspata Initiation and very necessary before moving from one level onto the next level.

Guidelines from Almine state that all initiates are to be mentored by a Master or Grand Master of Belvaspata. This ensures that each level of self-initiation is completed successfully. The mentor will assist you in preparing for self-initiation, answer any questions that you may have and also ensure that you are both competent and confident in working with Belvaspata. The mentor may issue a certificate stating that you have self-initiated and that they have mentored you. A directory of masters who may be contacted for mentoring may be found on the Belvaspata site, see the link at www.belvaspata.spiritualjourneys.com.

Note: *Belvaspata Angel Healing,* the recording that accompanies this book, was created to assist with learning the pronunciation of the language of the Infinite. It is not to be used for a session or for initiation. For self-initiation you must speak the Infinite's language of initiation for yourself.

 To obtain your copy of an MP3 download, please visit www.belvaspata.spiritualjourneys.com.

Preparing for Self-Initiation

1. Carefully study the material given in this book regarding Belvaspata.

2. Spend the necessary time studying and internalizing the appropriate material for the level of initiation you are preparing for.

    The 12 Pairs of Emotions for Level I

    The 16 Rays of Light for Level II

    The States of Being for Master Level

    The Heart Energies for Grand Master Level

3. Using the Alphabet of the Infinite Mother, translate the self-initiation ceremony. The language is written in vertical columns and written from left to right as shown on page 151.

4. Each initiation sigil is to be drawn on a separate piece of paper. The sigils are to be placed on or near the specified area of the body for each level of initiation.

5. When you are ready, you may lie down. Read the self-initiation ceremony out loud in the Infinite Mother's language. Draw each sigil in the air three times and call upon the angels of that sigil to place it in the appropriate area of your body three times. Read the translation and draw one sigil at a time.

6. When you are finished, close the initiation with the sigils for praise, love and gratitude by drawing them in the air above you.

7. Level I sigils are always used to open the initiation unless Level I and Level II are being done at the same time or Master and Grand Master are being done at the same time. In other words, if 2 levels of initiation are being done consecutively, it is only necessary to use Level I sigils for the first level, then continue on to the next level. Use of Level 1 sigils enhances receptivity for the initiation.

8. The original copy of your translation and sigils should be sent to the master who is mentoring you. They should keep them as a record if you wish to proceed on to self-initiate for other levels of Belvaspata. If this mentor is not available for subsequent initiations, send a copy of your previous translations and the date(s) when initiations were performed to the new mentor.

The Languages and Alphabet of Infinite Mother

Whatever is spoken in the languages of Mother/Infinite becomes reality. Having this power, the languages and their use constitute a most holy body of white and beneficial magic.

The purity of the languages makes them incapable of being misused. The use of them brings light and restores perfection. They are without doubt the most holy of symbols on earth.

The languages have appeared in 3 different forms in various cycles and have provided a guidance system for the cosmos. The choice of a specific language of the Mother/Infinite used during a given cycle of Creation provided the exact frequencies and amount of light needed at the time.

The Second Language of the Holy Mother
Used during the Cosmic Ascension
(Excerpted from *The Ring of Truth*)

Pronunciation of Mother's Language

The pronunciation is very much like German, other than that the 'v' (as in very) and 'w' (as in white) are pronounced as in English.

The syllables are pronounced individually when placed next to each other. There are no contracted sounds like 'au' (as in trauma). It would be necessary to say the 'a' and 'u' separately. The only exception to this rule is a double 'aa' at the end of a word. This indicates the 'a' sound (as in spa).

The 'ch' spelling at the beginning of a word is the only time it is pronounced as in 'church'. Everywhere else it is pronounced as in the German 'kirche' or somewhat like the Spanish x as in Mexico.

- 'u' is pronounced as in 'prudence'
- 'a' is pronounced as in 'garden'
- 'e' is as in 'pet'.
- 'i' is pronounced as in 'pink'
- 'o' is pronounced in the way someone with an English accent would say 'of' or 'cross'
- 'g' is always a hard 'g' like 'great'
- 'c' is always hard as in 'call'
- 'q' has a 'qw' sound as in 'queen'
- 'r' is slightly rolled—'rr'
- 'y' is pronounced as in 'Yvette', with an 'ee' sound

'I am happy' has a much higher frequency than 'I am tired', therefore 'I' and 'am' would be different in each of these sentences.

Also, when the concept is large, several words are needed. 'Beautiful' will have different words depending on what is described, but in each case the term will have several words since it is a complex concept.

There are no words for 'sad', 'pain', 'angry', 'protective' or 'fear', since those are illusory concepts in this creation of life. There are also no negative words.

'I' and 'we' would be the same word as this is a group consciousness language. Similarly, 'he' and 'they' would use the same word.

Sentences and Phrases:

1. *Aushbava heresh sishisim*
   Come here

2. *Va-aal vi-ish paru-es*
   Do it again

3. *Kre-eshna sa-ul varavaa*
   It is beautiful everywhere

4. *Pranuvaa sanuvesh vilsh-savu bravispa*
   We are with you when you think of us

5. *Aasushava pre-unan aruva bareesh*
   We come to open the gate

Note: 'Come' in this sense is not the same word used for 'come here'.

6. *Oonee varunish heshpiu tra barin*
   Everyone is dancing with joy

7. *Belesh bri anur bra vershpi iulan*
   Take away the frown from your face

8. *Nen hursh avervi tranuk averva?*
   When comes the moment of laughing?

Note: there is no word for time.

9. *Nun brash barnut pareshvi*
   Please take us with you

10. *Vursh venestu parneshtu*
    Magic is in the moment

11. *Iuvishpa niutrim sarem*
    Great things await

12. *Ruftravasbi iulem*
    Let the fun begin

13. *Verluash verurlabaa mi urla set viunish*
    Be prepared for the fulfilment of your dreams

14. *Be-ulahesh parve mi-ur ville starva*
    Speak to us through these sacred words

15. *Truaveshviesh aluvispaha maurnanuhe*
    Welcome to the fullness of our being

16. *Telech nusva rura vesbi*
    Through love are we connected

17. *Erluech spauhura vavish menuba*
    Find the new song that you sing

18. *Me-uhu vaubaresh ka-ur-tum*
    Our new dance is a joyous one

19. *Pelech parve uru-uhush vaspa pe-uravesh ple-ura*
    Together let us create wondrous moments

20. *Vala veshpa uvi kle-u vishpi ula usbeuf pra-uva*
    You are invited into the loving embrace of our arms

21. *Perenuesh krava susibreve truach*
    In great mercy you are renewed

22. *Pleshpaa vu skaura versebia nunuhesh*
    Allow your shoulders to feel lightness

23. *Verunachva ulusetvaabi manuresh*
    All are in this moment redeemed

24. *Keleustraha virsabaluf bra uvraha*
    You dwell in us and are ours

25. *Keleshpruanesh te le-usbaru*
    Call and we shall hear

Alphabet of the Holy Mother

1. AUX

2. PAH

3. GHEE

4. KA

5. G as in Gold

6. DJU as in Giraffe

7. B

8. PE as Peg

9. L

10. TRA

11. I as in Ink

12. N

13. R

14. A as in Far

15. M

16. E as in Leg

17. U as in True

18. V

19. SH

20. K

21. H

22. S

23. O as in Open

24. Y as in Yvette

25. QW as in Quail

26. T

27. CH as in Church

28. A as in Back

29. O as in Lock

30. XCH as in Mexico (Spanish pronunciation)

31. F

32. Z as in Azure (soft sound)

33. RR (rolled r)

34. P

35. Y as in Yes

36. CK (short K sound)

37. Period (placed at the end of a sentence)

38. Question Mark (placed at the beginning of a sentence)

Additional Letters
of Other Languages –
Used in the
Holy Mother's Languages

1. D

2. PF

3. KL

4. W

5. SHP

6. KRR

7. HF

8. PL

9. TL

Language of the Holy Mother

Magic is in the
moment.
*(Vursh venes-tu
parneshtu)*

Great things
await.
*(Iuvishpa
niutrim sarem)*

Let the fun
begin.
*(Ruftra-vasbi
iulem)*

Please take me
with you.
*(Nun brash
barnut pareshvi)*

Self-Initiation in the Language of the Infinite Mother

Prior to self-initiation into any specific level, ensure that you have completed translating the ceremony using the alphabet of the Infinite Mother and drawn each of the sigils on paper. This is an important and integral part of self-initiation. The preparation assists in raising your frequency for the initiation. (Hyphenation of the Sigil and Angel names is used to assist with pronunciation.)

Level I Belvaspata Initiation

Self-Initiation

Pelech vi brashvata urespi klaunash strechvi uklesva uhuru reshvi straunach Belvaspata.

By the power of the holy language, I enter into the Level 1 initiation of Belvaspata.

1. Uklesh varabi ukretnet **Rutsetviurubach** *u palva uheristat kletvubra. Kre stubava uset uvechvi kraunat valavish usta vabi uretvi* **Blautvapata** *pre nusvi haruhit.*

For the opening of my mind, I call in the angel **Rutsetvi-uru-bach**. By the power of his sigil, I instruct him to place the sigil of **Bla-utva-pata** three times in my forehead.

*2. Uklesh varabi ukretnet **Iornumubach** u varespi uheristat kletvubra. Kre stubava uset uvechvi kraunat valavish usta vabi varespi Kruvechpaururek pre nusvi haruhit.*

For the opening of my heart, I call in the angel **Iornumubach**. By the power of his sigil I instruct him to place the sigil of **Kru-vech-pa-uru-rek** three times in my heart.

*3. Uklesh varabi ukretnet **Truararirpleva** u stavavechspi umirarat. Kre stubava uset uvechvi kraunat valavish usta vabi pres pranatuk **Kelavisbavah** pre nusvi haruhit.*

For the receptivity of the body, I call in the angel **Tru-ararir-pleva**. By the power of his sigil I instruct him to place the sigil of **Kel-a-vis-ba-vah** three times within my navel.

Esta u manurch bria stuvaba reshvi straunach Belvaspata.

I am now in Level I Belvaspata.

Close by drawing the sigils for Praise, Love and Gratitude above the heart area or over the body.

Level II Belvaspata Initiation

Self-Initiation

Open the initiation with Level I initiation sigils unless Levels I and II are done together.

Pelech vi brashvata urespi klaunash strechvi uklesva basetvi reshvi straunach Belvaspata.

By the power of the holy language, I enter into the Level II initiation of Belvaspata.

*1. Uklesh varabi ukretnet **Krunechvaatruha** u stechvabi uleska bret net hurava. Kre stubava uset uvechvi kraunat valavish usta vabi perenutvi skaulag **Kelavisvauravech** pre nusvi haruhit.*

For the release of patterns that no longer serve, I call in the angel **Krunechva-atruha**. By the power of his sigil I instruct him to place the sigil of **Kel-a-visva-uravech** three times in my lower abdomen.

*2. Uklesh varabi ukretnet **Mirakluvael** u ste u plavaa urechspi hershstavaa uknech staura. Kre stubava uset uvechvi kraunat valavish usta vabi keres nusta-ava **Trechsubareshvi** pre nusvi haruhit.*

For the transmuting of matter to energy and then to light, I call in the angel **Mirakluvael**. By the power of his sigil I instruct him to place the sigil of **Trech-su-ba-reshvi** three times in my solar plexus.

*3. Uklesh varabi ukretnet **Kelevitraunar** u trana uruvet pre usta utvi us plavaa. Kre stubava uset uvechvi kraunat valavish usta vabi krunespi ustava **Patauruhutvi** pre nusvi haruhit.*

For the transfiguring of illusion to light, I call in the angel **Kelevi-traunar.** By the power of his sigil I instruct him to place the sigil of **Pata-uru-hutvi** three times in my sternum.

*4. Uklesh varabi ukretnet **Trechbaruruheresvi** u stavavechspi pre uhus traurat. Kre stubava uset uvechvi kraunat valavish usta vabi brat nutva rechspanadoch **Kersbaurveshpi** pre nusvi haruhit.*

For the sanctification of the body I call in the angel **Trechbar-uru-heresvi.** By the power of his sigil I instruct him to place the sigil of **Kers-baur-veshpi** three times in my crown.

*5. Uklesh varabi ukretnet **Vilivesbikeresna** u sta binavich steretu uvlaesh kletvubra. Kre stubava uset uvechvi kraunat valavish usta vabi stiekluava uprech vabi **Kletsutmanarech** pre nusvi haruhit.*

For the attracting of light into my voice, I call in the angel **Vilivesbi-keres-na.** By the power of his sigil I instruct him to place the sigil of **Klet-sut-manarech** three times in my throat.

*6a. Uklesh varabi ukretnet **Kruechnavilshpreva** u bestich haru vereshva kletvubra. Kre stubava uset uvechvi kraunat valavish usta vabi peresnustavat kliechspi **Visbelespahrechvi** pre nusvi haruhit.*

For the attracting of healing energies into my hands, I call in the angel **Kru-echna-vilshpreva.** By the power of his sigil I instruct him to place the sigil of **Vis-beles-pah-rech-vi** three times in my right hand.

*6b. Uklesh varabi ukretnet **Kruechnavilshpreva** u bestich haru vereshva kletvubra. Kre stubava uset uvechvi kraunat valavish usta vabi peresnustavat truvachspi **Visbelespahrechvi** pre nusvi haruhit.*

For the attracting of healing energies into my hands, I call in the angel **Kru-echna-vilshpreva.** By the power of his sigil I instruct him to place the sigil of **Vis-beles-pah-rech-vi** three times in my left hand.

*7. Uklesh varabi ukretnet **Kuuluvet** stau nenhurpersh ustachni versh u stanavach steraa. Kre stubava uset uvechvi kraunat valavish usta vabi tremish uretkla uvra vesti pelenuch ustechbi **Nenhershbikletrasut** pre nusvi haruhit.*

For the DNA activation of the codes of light, I call in the angel **Ku-ulu-vet.** By the power of his sigil I instruct him to place the sigil of **Nen-hersh-bi-klet-rasut** three times into my root chakra at the base of my spine.

*8. Uklesh varabi ukretnet **Belechhispavatra** ukresh mi hes vi ustachva plavaa. Kre stubava uset uvechvi kraunat valavish usta vabi sta u achva usbanadoch sterut **Veleechsbikluatret** pre nusvi haruhit. Uklesh baurabi ukretnet pehera **Kelipretvaha** tre u stamamit selbi usvi trevaa.*

For the creation of movement in light, I call in the angel **Belech-his-pavatra.** By the power of his sigil I instruct him to place the sigil of **Vele-echs-bi-kluatret** three times in the alpha chakra (one hand length below the base of the spine).

I ask that his wife **Keli-pret-vaha,** place the same sigil in the Earth.

*9a. Uklesh varabi ukretnet **Kretnauluvesbi** paurivi heshva ustevavi klasutbaru uraesh. Kre stubava uset uvechvi kraunat valavish usta vabi kresna stechvi kliechspi **Nunmerstararotbelchspi** pre nusvi haruhit.*

For bringing in the new template of frequency, I call in the angel **Kretna-ulu-vesbi.** By the power of his sigil I instruct him to place the sigil **Nun-mer-stararot-belch-spi** three times into the bottom of my right foot.

*9b. Uklesh varabi ukretnet **Kretnauluvesbi** paurivi heshva ustevavi klatsutbaru uraesh. Kre stubava uset uvechvi kraunat valavish usta vabi kresna stechvi truvachspi **Nunmerstararotbelchspi** pre nusvi haruhit.*

For bringing in the new template of frequency I call in the angel **Kretna-ulu-vesbi.** By the power of his sigil I instruct him to place the sigil **Nun-mer-stararot-belch-spi** three times into the bottom of my left foot.

Esta u vish basetvatu reshvi straunach Belvaspata esba unavespi stechmanarot ra utvaba kelesvi unus kraunata pre us ubarech.

I am now initiated into Level II of Belvaspata and connected to the planetary field to bring healing through the use of these sigils.

Close by drawing the sigils for Praise, Love and Gratitude above the heart area or over the body.

Master Level Belvaspata Initiation

Self-Initiation

Open the initiation with Level I initiation sigils.

Draw the Master Sigil above all the following parts of the body three times and in the order given. Say the name of the sigil, Bel-veres-nuk-vi, each time you draw it.

1. bottom of each foot
2. alpha chakra
3. root chakra
4. lower abdomen
5. navel
6. solar plexus
7. heart
8. sternum
9. throat
10. forehead
11. crown
12. both hands
13. 10" above crown

*Uklesh tre basetvi me uspata reshvi berek nautar Belvaspata, uklesh varabi ukretnet nautari spa uvechvi **Belveresnukvi.** Kre stubavat usetvi sta unava, **Urhetvi** kreunes tra va esta ulvavech ustavravi es bautra pre nusvi haruhit esbaerch usmi treur nun hesvata.*

Uset uvechvi steba kresna stechvi kliechspi esba u stau vi kresna stechvi truvachspi.Uset uvechvi steba achva usbanadoch sterut es vra tremish uretkla esva perenutvi skaulag. Uset uvechvi pres pranatuk es keres nustaava esva varespi esva krunespi ustava. Uset uvechvi steba stiekluava uprech vabi esba uretvi esba brat nutva rechspanadoch esba peresnustavat kliechspi esba peresnustavat truvachspi. Uset uvechvi steba stabalut.

Lahun estakva knues bra us ta uvi brat rechspanadoch. Parus na ta esva klua nu Lahun.

For my initiation into the Master Level of Belvaspata, I call in the angel of the master sigil, **Bel-veres-nuk-vi.** By the power of your sigil that I hold, **Urhetvi** come forth and place this sigil that connects me to the cosmic field three times in each of the centers I mention.

Place it into the bottom of my left foot and the bottom of my right foot. Place it into my alpha chakra, root chakra, lower abdomen, navel, solar plexus, heart, sternum, throat, forehead, crown, right hand and left hand. Place it into the tenth chakra ten inches above my crown, known as lahun.

Esta u vish basetvu reshvi pelevradoch ukles parva Belvaspata esbaur ne tru bravabit basetvi kluavanet perhet pra usva kliunesvi eshtra usbava Amanur.

Let all become one and one become all. I am now initiated as a Master of Belvaspata and am able to initiate others into this sacred healing modality given by the Goddess of Creation.

Close by drawing the sigils for Praise, Love and Gratitude above the heart area or over the body.

Grand Master Level Belvaspata Initiation

Self-Initiation

Open the initiation with Level I sigils unless Master and Grand Master initiations are done at the same time.

The Grand Master Sigil is drawn three times over the heart area and the name of the sigil is said three times — Kluagvanesvi-elu-achvraheresh-vi-skaulag.

Barach usta hesvi klanevuk staba urechspi utklasvaba utrenuch steravik peleshba utklenevriavak uhes stau va klau nas prava uhuresbi. Esklat us ste uvra klenevash pra uvra kelesnut verek stauvrabach usetvi minur pelesh **Bruakranuvigstelauachvraba, Kershheruvitpeleachuvespiklauna, Stuapruanatvikeleshna** *et kla ninur varset pre us veleshbi ukletvi bre* **Kluagvanesvieluachvrahereshviskaulag** *stunavek strau nas pra ve.*

Arvuklat vru elesbi sta minech staubileshvi usklaveres nesvabi ustech vre usbla eleshbi strau netvra stu velesbi nech tre ubrekva helesbi staravu. Kelvi arasva stu belechbi usta heresvri eshvra kluva vreshbi. Pre rech uvra nuresbi presatvi urla verleshvi Belvaspata kreunag viashva kluvanet **Kluagvanesvieluachvrahereshviskaulag** *pre usutvi treunag mi uresh priesva kleunich.*

As one who has practiced this sacred healing of the heart with respect and in honor of all life, I present myself to become a Grand Master practitioner. I call the angels, **Brua-kranuvig-stela-u-achvraba, Kersh-heruvit-pele-ach-uvespi-klauna** and **Stuapruanatvi-keleshna,** and by the authority of their sigils, instruct them to place the Grand Master sigil, **Kluagvanesvi-elu-achvrahereshvi-skaulag** three times in my heart center.

As Grand Master let them consecrate and initiate me, that I too may do so for others. Let my healing abilities increase one hundred fold. I am now a grand master of Belvaspata carrying the **Kluagvanesvi-elu-achvrahereshvi-skaulag** sigil within my heart.

Close by drawing the sigils for Praise, Love and Gratitude above the heart area or over the body.

Belvaspata Certificates of Initiations

The initiating Master or Grand Master may issue certificates upon completion of any level of Belvaspata initiation. Certificate templates may be purchased at office supply stores and online for creating certificates or create your own. An example of a certificate is in Appendix III.

Creating a word document template will allow you to insert the name, date, level of initiation and initiating master for each specific initiation. If all levels are completed, it is customary and acceptable to create only the Grand Master Level certificate.

The Belvaspata Directory

A directory of Masters and Grand Masters is located on our main Belvaspata website at www.belvaspata.spiritualjourneys.com.

Complete the following if you wish to be added to the directory:

1. Initiation or self-initiation into Master or Grand Master level of Belvaspata.
2. Submit a copy of an initiation certificate or a letter confirming initiation to jan@almine.net. Certificates and letters are to include the name of the initiate, level and date of initiation and signature of the initiator or mentor for self-initiation. All applications will be approved based on meeting these requirements.
3. Register on Spiritual Journeys store, click on Belvaspata link and Registration for Belvaspata Directory. (A small fee is charged to be listed on the directory.)

Note: Initiation into Belvaspata Master or Grand Master level along with daily practice for at least 6 months is required in order to register on the Belvaspata Directory.

PART VIII

Specialty Belvaspata Modalities

Introduction to Specialty Belvaspata Modalities

All levels of Belvaspata masters may use the sigils in the following sections of this Belvaspata manual without any further initiations. The Belvaspata Initiation and Healing Manual at the start of this book is a recommended reference and guide for the use of all Belvaspata modalities.

Any specialty Belvaspata may be used in conjunction with a basic Belvaspata session. Start with the initial session and then proceed with the specialty Belvaspata, unless otherwise directed. For example, Belvaspata for the Song of the Self is always done prior to a basic Belvaspata session or any other specialty Belvaspata.

General Guidelines for Performing Ceremonies

The following are general guidelines for performing ceremonies. If <u>specific</u> directions are provided for any ceremony, use those directions; otherwise follow these general guidelines.

Creating and Dismantling a Ceremonial Circle:

When creating a ceremonial circle, place the elements in a clockwise direction (on the floor or other surface). When dismantling the circle, pick up all the elements counter-clockwise.

Wheels, Squares, Triangles, Gates, etc as used in Ceremonies

When using elements such as Wheels, Triangles or Gates, the lowest numbers always go on top and the highest numbers on the bottom when these items are stacked. *Example:* Stack 1 is created at your head if you are lying down on your back or in front of your face if you are sitting. If each stack contains 8 Wheels then stack 1 contains Wheel 1–8 with lowest number on top and highest number on bottom; stack 2 contains Wheel 9–16, with lowest number on top and highest number on bottom — repeat this same order for each stack around the circle.

All ceremonial circles create an alchemical equation: Wheels or other items placed in stacks are created per the individual ceremony and create an alchemical equation that is different for each ceremony. Do not assume that you can determine the components of stacks for a ceremony with multiples of wheels, gates, etc.

The alchemy works through EACH item and thus it is important to stack them one upon another. This ensures that the components create the correct alchemical equation.

If the ceremony provides specific directions for creating stacks, follow them. All aspects of the alchemical equation have been considered by Almine as given in the specific instructions.

a. Item such as wheels, gates, squares, etc can be cut out singly. On some occasions when there are a large number of items, multiples may be placed on one page. As long as the elements are equally divided between the stacks and equally laid out on the pages — this is permissible. For example if there are 144 elements to be divided between 12 stacks, you may either have 2 elements per page or 4 elements per page. The types of elements should not be mixed when combining onto one page.

b. Ensure you follow the directions for creating the stacks needed for each of the ceremonies.

c. The shape of a circle must be maintained when creating the stacks.

d. If in doubt it is best to follow the exact ceremonial guidelines as given.

e. *With our intent to create the sacred space, we are part of the alchemical equation.* When following the ceremonial guidelines, we produce the known results of the alchemical equation that are intended for any specific ceremony.

Position

Lying down on your back is the preferred position. You may use a bed, a massage table or the floor. Ensure you are comfortable. It is okay to use a small pillow under your knees and your head or neck.

Follow the directions as given for each specific ceremony. For the majority of these ceremonies, your head should be placed at the Number 1 Wheel or Stack (which correlates to 12 on the clock). If you choose to sit on a chair, the Number 1 Wheel or Stack should be placed in front of you.

Creating Sacred Space

Avoid interruptions of any sort as you create your sacred space and participate in your ceremony, whether it is a physical ceremony or one of intent. Once you start the ceremony it is best to complete it. (Unplug the phone, go to the restroom, etc - prior to starting.)

Ceremonies build upon each other. It is recommended that they be completed in the order given. Ceremonies may be repeated as often as you feel is appropriate and right for you.

Note: Maintain the sacred space and circle — keep animals and children out of the area by closing doors, etc. The frequency of the sacred circle is affected by their presence and they are affected by the ceremonial frequencies. These frequencies may be too high for them.

Recommendations during pregnancy: The frequencies of a ceremony may be too high for the baby and therefore, not comfortable. As a general rule, avoid doing ceremonies during pregnancy.

The Use of Wheels

A wheel is a visual image that conveys non-cognitive, sacred and empowering information. They are similar to gateways through which specific healing frequencies are drawn and are power sources in the same way a holy object would be.

The wheels are alive and as we work with them they provide us with deep insights into the vastness and wealth of our own being, reminding us of all that we are.

Each wheel is a stand-alone wheel and can be used by itself. When wheels are used in a sequence, they tell a story and combine to make an equation.

Mystical practices have a beginning and a closure. If you are working with a sequence of wheels, do not stop in the middle as it leaks resources and energy. For this reason it is important that you always complete each sequence.

To access the information contained within the wheels at a deeper level you may place your hands on the wheels or run your hand across them — the left hand is receptive and the right hand promotes understanding.

Lying down, you may also place a wheel at your feet and upon contemplating its meaning, bring it up through your body from your feet to the Lahun Chakra 10 inches above your head. If a wheel feels 'stuck' anywhere, continue to feel the quality of the wheel until it moves freely. If you are working with a sequence of wheels, ensure that the highest numbered wheel is at the bottom and the lowest numbered wheel is at the top. Work with one wheel at a time and fully integrate one before moving on to the next. As you do, also contemplate how the qualities of each wheel combine and complement the other wheels within the sequence.

Possible Uses for Wheels include:
- Meditate on a wheel.
- Place on the walls of a healing space, office or a room in which you spend a lot of time.
- With intention they can be placed into the body or placed directly on the body.
- Specific wheels can be placed under a healing table when working on someone or under a chair that you frequently sit on.
- Create your own personal mandala that you carry with you.

Wheel for the Angels of Love, Praise and Gratitude

Love - **Neresh-huspata**

Praise - **Blavit-rechvatu**

Gratitude - **Nusarat-ubesvi**

Photos of Blessings Received in a Retreat with The Seer Almine

Light emanates as a ball around the
Seer Almine and a student.

Photos of Blessings Received in a Retreat with The Seer Almine

Note the light emanating from the student's chest.

Photograph of an Angelic Appearance during a retreat with the Seer Almine

An angelic presence lights up the room as students visit the Seer's home.

Book II

Kaanish Belvaspata
Healing Modality of Enlightenment

Introduction to Kaanish Belvaspata

During the final quarter of 2008, I was instructed by the Infinite to prepare 14 different websites — each containing the equivalent of at least half a book of information, freely available to all. Deep mystical techniques were given from many ancient and sacred traditions — many of which had over the eons either lost their potency and power or their purity.

The purpose for this renaissance of incorruptible and powerful information had not been clear to me until the first week of February 2009. For the first time, Belvaspata and other previously separate bodies of information started weaving together. The restoration of the mastery and incorruptible magic to man that is his birthright seemed to be the overall purpose.

During the last week of January 2009, information was received from the angels that led me to discover a huge compound of pyramids and towers, connected by circular tunnels. The angels had built the structure, with the assistance of a group known as the Zhong-galabruk (the Cat people).

Shortly after receiving Kaanish Belvaspata, the Belvaspata of Enlightenment, another marriage of information took place:

Belvaspata sigils to use with the complete Toltec body healing system. Yet again there was an integration of two entirely separate healing modalities for greatly enhanced results.

It is clear that the age of empowerment of those who have wished to render service in purity and with power has dawned. The tools are in our hands. Angels have been called to assist us. With dedication in our hearts, let us embrace the spiritual maturity we have earned and truly become the light beacons of the Earth.

To the Infinite One Life the Glory Forever,

Almine

The Seer Almine Receives a
Scroll of Ancient Records

Almine has been photographed in various locations as she receives scrolls, which she later translates and shares with her students. The scrolls, which appear on her head, are seen in this interdimensional photo taken at a retreat in Sedona, Arizona, 2010.

The Sigil for Kaanish Belvaspata

Kaaresh Sabahuch Neseta

Kaanish Belvaspata

The Healing Modality of Enlightenment
(Literal translation: the cosmic proxy Belvaspata)

With the advent of this Belvaspata, a few notable changes have occurred:

Firstly, Master and Grand Master initiations may be performed simultaneously. Secondly, this unique form of Belvaspata, representing the high mind, has come forth to be used by qualified masters of Belvaspata at all levels.

- Level I and Level II Belvaspata masters represent the healing of the sub-conscious or low mind.
- Practitioners of Master and Grand Master Levels represent the healing of the middle-mind (the left and right brain).
- The Kaanish Belvaspata is the healing modality representing the high mind.

How does it work?

Every sigil of Kaanish Belvaspata represents the cosmos. When used by a Belvaspata master of any level, the recipient is a proxy for the cosmic well-being. Such great service must be compensated for by dramatic increases in consciousness.

When it is used, which can be done as part of a usual Belvaspata session or as a separate session to benefit cosmic life, the recipient will also reap physical benefits. There does not need to be an ailment for Kaanish Belvaspata to be done.

The gift of physical healing regular Belvaspata brings is now supplemented by the advent of Kaanish Belvaspata as an enhancer of consciousness.

Are Initiations required to perform it?

The only initiations that are necessary are the initiations or self-initiations that regular Belvaspata masters undergo. As always it is requested that you credit Almine as the originator of this profound work designed to set man free from illusion.

Using Kaanish Belvaspata as a stand-alone Session

1. Open the session with an expansion process and hold the expanded awareness for as long as you feel is appropriate. For example 5–10 minutes may be sufficient.

2. Proceed with Kaanish Belvaspata. Draw the sigils as you feel guided either in the air or trace them in the book. Remember the intent of this modality is purification and enlightenment and it is not created to address healing or any specific problem.

3. Always close the session by signing the sigils for praise, love and gratitude as this materializes the healing intentions and pulls awareness in.

Note: Prior to doing a session with a client, it is important that you, as the practitioner, have completed all 5 levels of Kaanish Belvaspata and integrated all the wheels at least once. It is not required that the client integrate the wheels.

The Illusions that Fractured the DNA of Man

The Formation of the Rose

The following is an excerpt from month 1
of Almine's online course, *The Science of Alchemy*.
(See www.spiritualjourneys.com for online courses.)

The rose pattern, indicating the sound or frequency chambers of the DNA of man, is the kaleidoscope lens mentioned as part of the seven illusions later in the book. The cosmic sound chambers are the reflection of the Infinite's DNA and follow a similar pattern.

In the last few days of January 2009, the answers to healing the separation consciousness of man found in his DNA presented itself. A body of information called Kaanish Belvaspata was received: a healing modality to bring enlightenment.

But the way in which it brings enlightenment was not initially clear as the first 14 hours of information was transcribed. It was only during the last 10 hours, which came a few days later, that a pattern started to reveal itself: we were healing the illusions that fractured the DNA of man, restoring its pristine nature.

This is why it was emphatically stressed to me that the steps to be followed when doing Kaanish Belvaspata had to be done in the order given. The DNA strand has to be healed, its fractured petals blended into one from the inside out. The effect of writing down the sigils and angels was profound. The light in the room was golden then white. My hands seemed transparent and sometimes the pen as well — a truly magnificent experience.

The New Expanded and Enhanced Rose DNA Template

Healing the Rows of Petals in the DNA Rose

Enlightenment Levels I and II

The research of many behavioral scientists has indicated that man seems to have a 'pain body' — a layer of magnetic frequencies that carry memories of pain. This resembles the memory of someone's voice on the magnetic strip of an audiotape that can be replayed over and over again.

During 2008 a great deal had been done by the Infinite to remove the memory of separation by eliminating the electrical grids of the cosmos, as well as the matrices. But the cosmic pain body, the magnetic matrix, had not been dissolved.

The pain body originates from the DNA strand, where it lies like a surrounding sheath of magnetic frequencies containing memories of pain and trauma. The first two levels remove this.

Enlightenment Level III

This level clears rows 3, 7, 12 and 20 of the petals of the DNA rose of their separations by dispelling the core illusions that caused them in the first place.

Row of 3 petals
For the removal of the illusions of space, duality and polarity.

Row of 7 petals
For the removal of the 7 cosmic illusions of the mirror, the rainbow, the echo, the mirage, the lens, the kaleidoscope lens and the cosmic vacuum created by clustering as a way to create.

Row of 12 petals
These sigils remove the 7 shadow casters of inaccessible potential, wisdom, the fractured DNA, traditions and nationalism forming soul patterns, the illusion of external information, the building blocks of life and the illusion of accomplishment.

Row of 20 petals
The last portion of level III corrects illusions around the perfection of life's unfoldment; the illusion of the mistakes of life. The misperceptions removed are:
1. That life's stressors make some stronger but are more than others can bear, causing them to 'crack', and that there are victims of too much stress
2. That we have been conditionally loved, approved only when we are 'good'
3. That we are imperfectly made and then punished if we do not succeed
4. That we should have more abilities than what we do have
5. That Creation is formed through trial and error
6. That the purpose of Creation is for the Infinite to learn and experience the discovery of Its Being
7. That there are flaws in the timing of when certain things happen

Enlightenment Level IV

The Row of 33 Petals
For the removal of the 3 primary causes of victimhood:

The illusions
1. That unfairness and inequity exist
2. That we are exploited or used as a resource by the Infinite
3. That the cosmos is haphazardly or inexpertly handled

The Row of 54 Petals
The sigils related to this portion eliminate the seven causes of hopelessness:
1. That we are given unfair standards to live by
2. That the pace is too fast or too slow
3. That there is an unfair amount of responsibility placed on us
4. That life is part of a tyrannical system with not enough allowance for us to self-express
5. That there are unrealistic expectations of us
6. That we're blocked from flourishing rather than supported
7. Life is to be endured rather than enjoyed

The Row of 72 Petals
This eliminates the three primary causes of fear:
1. Fear of failure through inadequacy
2. Fear of missing something we should know or do
3. Fear of not seeing and / or making the right choices

The Row of 96 Petals

This final section of Level IV eliminates the seven causes of agony that lie as obsolete programming in the DNA:

1. The illusion that we can be separated from what we love
2. Feelings of being misplaced, as though we don't belong here
3. Feeling there should be an end to the journey
4. Living on the edge, vulnerable, as though bad things could happen at any time
5. Feeling that home is an external place
6. Feeling that we don't have a place where our unique gifts can be expressed, appreciated or understood
7. Feeling unprotected against harm

Enlightenment Level V

<u>The Row of 144 Petals</u>

This portion instills the 3 attitudes of surrender:

1. Surrendering to the moment
2. Taking full responsibility for what we manifest in our environment
3. Surrendering to our inner guidance

<u>The Row of 207 Petals</u>

There is only one extremely powerful sigil for the wholeness of the self through the embodiment of the 144 Self Wheels.

<u>The Row of 333 Petals</u>

There is only one sigil for the embodiment of inner peace and contentment. This sigil creates the embodiment of the 4 Wheels of Inner Peace.

The Four Wheels of Inner Peace

1. Delighting in the flow of change
2. Living in the light of complete self-honesty
3. Living in perfect harmonious inner integration
4. Finding a cherishing inner home

<u>The Row of 459 Petals</u>

There is one sigil for the embodying of the Thirteen Wheels of the Manifestation of Mastery.

13 Wheels of Manifestation of Mastery
1. Letting our light shine to the fullest
2. Expecting miracles with hearts of hope
3. Acknowledging our Divine Heritage as Creations of the Infinite
4. Embracing our Divine Perfection
5. Seeing our beauty and majesty reflected in nature
6. Knowing all life lives within us
7. Claiming all knowledge and effortless knowing
8. Living in the sovereignty of self-expression
9. Taking full responsibility for the quality of each moment
10. Living with the glory of elegance
11. Pleasing our heart first, that giving may come from fullness
12. Dedicating our lives to being the embodiment of Immortal Glory
13. Living each moment majestically

Summary: When the partitions of the Rose's petals are removed, we live in total oneness — the God-kingdom. The One Wheel That Contains All symbolizes this and is the design found on the floor of a massive and complex compound of angel magic (known as the Wheel of Life). The nucleus of the DNA has become one with all the petals.

From the Library of the Angels

The DNA of all races combine in that of man
Like the ends of many strings he holds in his hands
Tablets of light, written in gold
Shall bring man powers of angels to hold

A few shall stand forth, with love in their hearts
Then great changes among men shall start
As systems destructure and tyranny fails
Hope they will bring of a better way

No more shall men labor while only a few gain
Angel sigils shall heal humankind's pain
When all wavers, succumb not to fear
Call through the angels and assistance is near

PART II

Kaanish Belvaspata

Kaanish Belvaspata

Enlightenment Level I

Paara-hiruvat

The angel for fluid and graceful change through
Kaanish Belvaspata Level I

Note: Before starting Level I, Kaanish Belvaspata,
look at the sigil of the angel for fluid and graceful
change. Call the name of the angel and say:

*By the power of your sigil that I hold, I call on you to
create a fluid and graceful process of purification and
enlightenment through Level I of Kaanish Belvaspata.*

Angel name:
1. Belshi-etprevaa-harustraa   Kiresparvi

For the healing of the subconscious mind

Angel name:
2. Pluhat-verbis-uvastaba   Nu-avesbi

For the healing of the middle mind

Angel name:
3. Krach-bahar-ustaba   Nunaveshbi-strauhar

For the healing of the higher mind

In Kaanish Belvaspata all sigils are proxy sigils, in that they are automatically done for the cosmos – thereby blessing the person giving and receiving (all) with gifts of enlightenment.

4. Plihabak-velvesh-aruna

Angel name:

Kistebaruk

For the balancing of masculine and feminine components in mind

5. Bru-abak-setlvi

Angel name:

Kurasastrava

For clear communication between electrical and magnetic components within mind and the body

6. Vrubranik-salvavesbi

Angel name:

Establanish-veravi

For the unconditional oneness of all minds

7. Kelhavi-skavel-urespavi

Angel name:
Nichtunenheshvi

For the opening of mind to Infinite Presence

8. Virut-helvis-estravaa

Angel name:
Klunechbashbi

For clarity of awareness

9. Spu-aretnushet-vavi

Angel name:
Agnasta-bluavet

For establishing reference points during expansion

10. Kuha-avasta-pli-aha

Angel name:
Kinesta-plava

For removing fear for survival from the middle mind

11. Tru-bilechspa-kabelhut

Angel name:
Ustrava

For removing fear for survival from the sub-conscious mind

12. Vrupalik-stuanut-vestabi

Angel name:
Nunasbi

For removing fear for survival from internal organs

13. Kaalsh-hik-servatu

Angel name:
Eres-tranunit

For removing the constrictive response from muscles

14. Kurutbalas-vershvabi

Angel name:
Michpa-nunetvi

For instilling humor into the muscle groups to promote surrender

15. Paartlhut-skluvechva

Angel name:
Mishvel-splara

For removing the tendency of joints to lock,
as an emergency response

16. Blu-anushpavaa-hesvi

Angel name:
Kinig-stetvi

To remove the fight or flight response from internal organs

17. Kluvaruk-erestava

Angel name:
Biletrekvi

To remove the fight or flight response from muscles

18. Kurutnunestu

Angel name:
Pli-eshbrakbi

To remove fight or flight response from joints

19. Kaaretnunherspaa

Angel name:
Pitribilechskla

To remove the memory of traumatic creation from the heart

---

20. Kaararat-arasnanat-vavi

Angel name:
Ustubalechvi

To remove fear of the unknown from the mind

---

21. Aaras-bravabish-huvra

Angel name:
Kilsatvavi

To remove from the memory of traumatic creation from the cells

22. Paarisvit-skubalva

Angel name:
Tru-esbi

To remove the impulse to constrict from the stomach

23. Kaarutsalvavi

Angel name:
Neshpata

To remove fear of our vastness from the high mind

24. Baalich-bravabu

Angel name:
Kaanish-vavet-uruha

To create the optimum ratio of density in the body

25. Akanavush-erespa

Angel name:
Klanek-vravu-savuta

To dissolve bodily matrices and static patterns of obsolete reactions

26. Pluhas-estaval

Angel name:
Nunanesh-usetvi

To create a frame of reference between our heart
and the Infinite during our expansion

27. Kaarachselvi-nurusta

Angel name:
Tri-eshlava

To establish the optimum performance of the body's resources

28. Kursetni-uklesh

Niklesvi

To enhance power and energy within physical matter

29. El-klaresh-spi-uva

Angel name:
Nisetbla-uvu

The equal distribution of bodily resources
through the activation of inner morality

30. Bibavet-uselvavi

Angel name:
Araspratlva

The restoration of innocence to inner and outer senses

Angel name:

31. Kurachbirat-havrusta   Ninachvi

To remove illusory frequencies from the body

Angel name:

32. Kaarsat-barestruha   Gilgal-vileshvi

To open the unified field of the minds to Infinite Presence

FOR ALZHEIMER'S DISORDER:

Use sigils 1-7 plus sigils 33, 34 and 35.
The use of sigils 8 and 9 may also be of help for someone exhibiting Alzheimer's.

AUTISM:

The same sigils can also be used for autism, as well as sigils 8 and 9.

33. Nusta-erechvrahur

Angel name:
Vilives-pahur

For the removal of heavy metals from the brain

34. Kariknuspavaa

Angel name:
Kurutprahe

For the strengthening of the lymphatic system

35. Berek-pratlhut

Angel name:
Suhuvatvata

For the delivering of oxygen to the energy producing
organelles of brain cells

36. Kirit-nuvech-spavi

Angel name:
Brivach-sabuta

For the removal of all discordance

37. Kluhavech-spavi

Angel name:
Estrevananu-hash

For the revelation of absolute truth and clarity

38. Kaanish-serbatu

Angel name:
Unechsvi-harvuta

For the removal of fear of survival

39. Baarasavut-elekvi

Angel name:
Kiristrava-vilines

For the restoration of angelic powers to man

40. Kaalech-uvasta-sevetvi

Angel name:
Sitri-manunesh

For the restoration of the abilities to do high magic in human DNA

41. Paalchva-nenubush-sparura

Angel name:
Pitri-nanunet

For the ability to work with alchemy of light in healing

42. Trubabesvek-keleshni

Angel name:
Tru-esvi-besbi

For the ability to work with alchemy of frequency in healing

43. Trabiliknis-uhastra

Angel name:
Vristech-biristaa

For the removal of patterns of emergency

44. Fraternuk-steveliva

Angel name:
Klugava

For harmony and full co-operation in light

45. Pelish-ustra-nenavish

Angel name:

Klugavi-ugranot

For the harmonious frequencies of peace

Kaanish Belvaspata

Enlightenment Level II

Glu-ava-uruhit

The angel for fluid and graceful change through
Kaanish Belvaspata Level II

Note: Before starting Level II, Kaanish Belvaspata,
look at the sigil of the angel for fluid and graceful
change. Call the name of the angel and say:

*By the power of your sigil that I hold, I call on you to
create a fluid and graceful process of purification and
enlightenment through Level II of Kaanish Belvaspata.*

1. Kinash-setvevu-aranach

Angel name:
Stiblnesvi

For rebirthing the self with love and respect

2. Kunash-helesvi-spechva

Angel name:
Kininash-shelvavi

For inspired self-parenting

3. Ninushet-belechvi-harusta

Angel name:
Kishat-anesvi

For the complete dissolving of the magnetic matrix
(the 'pain' body)

4. Kavavish-unesvi-servevaa

Angel name:
Mishpi-he-reva

For joyous re-union into Oneness

5. Michmishet-nestu-servetut

Angel name:
Pi-iharestat

For the reclaiming of the wholeness of self

6. Nichtaa-uklesvi-selvuvaa

Angel name:
Keenash-heresvi

For the flourishing of abundant life

7. Kuchbarach-nashte-perut-haruva

Angel name:
Nistuperevu

For the receiving of exponential insights

8. Nuchpa-seretu-suvetvi

Angel name:
Mishivet-peres

For complete inner peace and unconditional oneness

9. Kunus-paresva-kinushta-uvechvi

Angel name:
Kru-anetvi-selveva

For functioning from the fullest DNA strand capacity

10. Kru-avas-tranadoch-pilesha

Angel name:
Uselvi-here-nat

For self-forgiveness through compassionate understanding

---

11. Arasnusetvila-vra-ur-tra-unes

Angel name:
Petri-bilebach

For the full and equitable restoration of resources

---

12. Nus-strech-uhus-pananech

Angel name:
Klihe-selvatu

For the removal of the illusion of external geometry

13. Kli-iheves-ubech-sta-uva

Angel name:
Nisti-bile-bach

For the removal of the illusion of loss

14. Mishet-ninesvu-kalisva

Angel name:
Kruve-pli-esh-narusta

For the removal of cyclical and repetitive patterns in cosmic life

15. Sitlhur-skaluva-neshvi

Angel name:
Paranut-uskelvi

For the restoration of self-determination and sovereignty

16. Brubas-natvi-skalech-piresh-haresvi

Angel name:
Klua-bak-belesvi

For inner support and the activation and
contribution of inner well-being

---

17. Kirchva-nenusv-tra-uva

Angel name:
Skalesh-bilesva

The healing and implementation of skipped developmental stages

---

18. Minesh-trekbar-selvuva

Angel name:
Nusbak-heresut

For the complete elimination of harmful experimentation

19. Kaalchverbret-sesatchvi-kerunet

Angel name:
Pli-erek-veresta

For the belief that progress is easily accomplished
and self-belief in our ability to succeed

20. Kunash-petruvi-haresva

Angel name:
Kelsetvi-varuha

For the removal of memory blocks of that which is

21. Parash-urek-sevuvi

Angel name:
Trinesvi-arurat

For the removal of memories of that which is not

22. Kinesh-paravi

Angel name:

Kersvi-eru-nat

For the removal of all forms of dictatorships

23. Stubaru-eretvi

Angel name:

Kluvas-pi-retvi

For the balancing of all stagnation, atrophy and hyper-activity

24. Nunash-erklat-vrabish

Angel name:

Ninsur-per-het-varesva

For the full ability to have and interpret all perspectives

25. Kerich-verna-servatu

Keenash-vitvi

For reclaiming Sovereignty of effective expression

26. Plubesh-estavi-nes-habasta

Pirhut-pratlvi

For establishing a relationship with impeccable power

27. Kaaru-selvi-ubesvi

Kuras-stret-vi

For healing feelings of abandonment by power

28. Kerash-prehu-satva-unash

Angel name:

Krikenet-uluhur

For trust in Infinite Guidance and being heard

29. Mishtave-piranukvi

Angel name:

Stuchva-subavet

For the removal of the illusion of fatigue

30. Virsat-eleklu-vileshvi

Angel name:

Nachsta-minuvir

For perpetual self-regeneration and rejuvenation

31. Mishpa-heruhit-ustatvi

Angel name:
Kinashvet-ruvi

For removing all psychological bondage from expectations

32. Kaaresh-steravu-kinachvi

Angel name:
Pla-ater-brubashvi

For removing all compensatory behavior patterns

33. Kaarsbak-stetvaa-uvaster

Angel name:
Kluhuva-eresbi

For complete trust in the perfection of the One Life

Kaanish Belvaspata

Enlightenment Level III

Paarabush-Hersevat

The angel for fluid and graceful change through
Kaanish Belvaspata Level III

Note: Before starting Level III, Kaanish Belvaspata,
look at the sigil of the angel for fluid and graceful
change. Call the name of the angel and say:

*By the power of your sigil that I hold, I call on you to
create a fluid and graceful process of purification and
enlightenment through Level III of Kaanish Belvaspata.*

1. **Erech-tranavich-hurespa**

Angel name:
Kirivabesbi

For the complete dissolving of the illusion of space

2. **Birispak-unesvi-haras-stat**

Angel name:
Estava-bireshbi

For the complete dissolving of duality

3. **Kinavi-selvavu-urasbi**

Angel name:
Kluhava-ste-vavi

For the complete dissolving of polarity

4. Kelvabi-estabi-minuvach

Angel name:
Nechstach-va-vi-hereshva

For the complete dissolving of the four illusions of light[8]

5. Klubaset-neshbahur

Angel name:
Pitri-balusva-hereshvi

For the complete dissolving of the illusions of sound
(the echo and the soundless vacuum)

6. Nichtu-servatet

Angel name:
Kilesti-haruvar

For the complete assimilation of potential

7. Pelesh-vrihar-salvustet

Angel name:
Nunesh-urechsti

For the elimination of the wisdom of past experience

8. Biritbek-giritna-selvavu

Angel name:
Pruvetsklaba

For the complete elimination of separation
in the chambers and strands of DNA

9. Nuchter-servu-eleshar

Angel name:
Glaneeshservatu

For the formation of a unified DNA field

10. Nusba-erestu-klanivespa

Angel name:
Palech-nenestu

For the elimination of traditional and racial templates in soul-force[9]

11. Kluvirit-stachvavi-nesva

Angel name:
Uvabechspi

For the dissolving of the illusion of separation and
and the existence of the building blocks of life

12. Bli-esh-uret-plihek-ustava

Angel name:
Minavech-spereru

For the dissolving of the illusion of accomplishments of the dream

13. Niklesh-baruchspi

Angel name:
Kluvechsbi-arurash

For the elimination of the illusion of the
existence of external information

14. Keenash-virabak

Angel name:
Nuchsperaa

For the removal of the belief that unfair stress can cause
life-forms to fail to live their highest potential

15. Unech-vribesh-erenut

Angel name:
Kilinesvabek

For the removal of the belief that the Infinite loves conditionally
and punishes if we don't meet expectations

16. Klanavish-steravu

Angel name:
Nuchstavru-skelavich

For the removal of the belief that we are imperfectly made, causing us to suffer or not live up to the highest potential

17. Kaanek-vishvabaa-erurek

Angel name:
Nichtu-ser-vavu

For the removal of the belief that Creation is based on trial and error

18. Kenuva-pirithur-selvuva-vechbi

Angel name:
Kelsit-heresba

For the removal of the belief that the purpose of Creation is so that the Infinite might learn about Its own existence

19. Nuchtavu-skelesva

Angel name:
Unesbi-skala-lot

For the removal of the belief that we should have
more abilities at any specific moments

20. Kisahur-pilit-vribach-eruvi

Angel name:
Kilich-birit-verbaa

For the removal of the belief that any flaw in
the timing of manifestation can exist

Kaanish Belvaspata

Enlightenment Level IV

Pilish-herset-varukla

The angel for fluid and graceful change through
Kaanish Belvaspata Level IV

Note: Before starting Level IV, Kaanish Belvaspata,
look at the sigil of the angel for fluid and graceful
change. Call the name of the angel and say:

*By the power of your sigil that I hold, I call on you to
create a fluid and graceful process of purification and
enlightenment through Level IV of Kaanish Belvaspata.*

Angel name:

1. Kiris-barabak-ustanve-mishet   Kiristat-ve

For the removal of the belief that unfairness and inequity can exist

---

Angel name:

2. Kilikhur-subatve   Erestahutvi

For the removal of the belief that the Infinite exploits
and uses us for Its own purpose

Angel name:

3. Paarish-bravek-salvuvet-anish   Klugvaba-ineshvi

For the removal of the belief that the Cosmos is run in an inept
way or that there is something the Infinite does not know

4. Kaalistar-urvavi-unachsvi

Angel name:
Kurunut-stelvavi

For the removal of the illusion of the Infinite
measuring us by unfair standards

5. Mishtel-blavuch-steravi

Angel name:
Unashvi-heresta

For the removal of the illusion of the Infinite
requiring us to grow at an unfair pace

**6. Nishtar-blahep-ustava-
kanunish**

Angel name:
Silvevi-erestar-nachvi

For the removal of the illusion of the responsibility
placed upon us being too heavy

Angel name:

7. Kelech-vibrish-harnustat   **Nichstor-balashvi**

For the removal of the illusion that Cosmic Life is a tyrannical system that does not allow for self-expression

Angel name:

8. Aralesh-mispi   **Ku-uhuret-spavi**

For the removal of the illusion that the Infinite has unrealistic expectations of us

Angel name:

9. Kaaratvi-uranesh-staruvi   **Karas-uvra-hespi**

For the removal of the illusion that Cosmic Life blocks us, rather than promoting our flourishing

10. Pelespravi-usetvi

Angel name:
Kiritna-uhelesh-bi

For the removal of the illusion that life is
to be endured rather than enjoyed

11. Kaalichba-ninustreva-piritvi

Angel name:
Gaalech-pritvaa

For the removal of fear of failure through inadequacy

12. Kubalva-utrechvi-staruva

Angel name:
Stubaret-unurasvi

For the removal of fear of missing what we should know or do

13. Kaanish-mechspa-meruhit

Angel name:

Kalsva-erut-trahe

For the removal of the fear of not seeing
and making the right choice

14. Kulchba-merurit-skalvava

Angel name:

Kuranat-valshpi

For the removal of the illusion that we can
be separated from what we love

15. Ustret-bileshba-astavu

Angel name:

Estre-mirash-piravit

For the removal of the feeling that we are misplaced;
that we can be anywhere we don't belong

16. Kunish-pretpraha-usitveresva

Angel name:
Nukvi-ster-avet

For the removal of the illusion that we
have an end to our journey of life

17. Skalikvich-suvavetvi

Angel name:
Kilash-pratu-var

For the removal of feeling as though we are in a state
of emergency because bad things may happen

18. Brubasput-uknachbi

Angel name:
Kiritnasv-uravet

For the removal of the illusion that home is an external place

19. Heretprabush-pravaa

Angel name:
Usalvavi-knichva

For the removal of the illusion of feeling our
unique gifts are not valued nor understood

20. Kaa-avubrit-pelish-vabraa

Angel name:
Kaanish-veles-bra

For the removal of the feeling of being unprotected against harm

Kaanish Belvaspata

Enlightenment Level V

Kunash-birushva

The angel for fluid and graceful change through
Kaanish Belvaspata Level V

Note: Before starting Level V, Kaanish Belvaspata,
look at the sigil of the angel for fluid and graceful
change. Call the name of the angel and say:

*By the power of your sigil that I hold, I call on you to
create a fluid and graceful process of purification and
enlightenment through Level V of Kaanish Belvaspata.*

1. Nustechvi-velebra-hasvi

Angel name:
Kalabi-suvavet

For the attitude of surrendering to the moment

2. Eretkle-uhurabish

Angel name:
Selvavi-pireshnuravet

For the attitude of taking full responsibility for the environment

3. Keenasat-plubakvi-erutprave

Angel name:
Kelsut-manavech

For the attitude of surrendering to inner guidance

Angel name:

4. Graanik-spelebaa-skechvi   Vilshkrabi-minhursat

For the complete wholeness of self through the
implementation of the 144 Self Wheels[8]

Angel name:

5. Kilinat-esvavi-nusba   Grunik-ustatvi

For inner contentment and peace through
embodying the 4 Wheels of Inner Peace[9]

Angel name:

6. Selva-nusvi-sklaurach-uhelasvi Pitirach-ushel-vi

For the embodying of the 13 Wheels of Manifestation of Mastery[10]

---

1 See the section on 144 Self Wheels.
2 See the section on the 4 Wheels of Inner Peace.
3 See the section on the 13 Wheels of the Manifestation of Mastery.

THE ONE THAT CONTAINS ALL

THE WHEEL OF THE GOD KINGDOM'S SIGILS[11]

Angel name:

7. Kenesh-pararuknichverti-uselvaa

Stuvabechsbinusurubach

For the complete synchronization of our environment with the perfection of our individuation.
Let me embody The One Wheel That Contains All[12.]

---

4 For further information on the god-kingdom, see Secrets of the Hidden Realms (The Evolutionary Stages of Man).
5 See the One Wheel that Contains All, page 340.

Closing Sigils

Praise

Love

Gratitude

PART III

The Wheels of
Kaanish Belvaspata

Integrating the Wheels of Kaanish Belvaspata

The directions given below apply to the Self Wheels, Wheels of Inner Peace and the Wheels of the Manifestation of Mastery.

All of the wheels of Kaanish Belvaspata are to be integrated at least once as one begins to use it. It's not necessary that the wheels be integrated for each session, or required that the wheels be placed at the feet during a session. The directions below explain how to integrate the wheels.

1. If you are working with one wheel—look at the wheel and when you feel guided close you eyes and 'feel' the wheel within you. You may also use either your left hand to increase you receptivity of the qualities of the wheel or your right hand to increase you understanding of its qualities.

To work with a sequence of wheels create a stack with the lowest numbered wheel on top and the highest numbered wheel at the bottom. Place the stack at your feet where you will be lying. It would be advisable to hold this book beside you so you can both look at the wheel and read its name.

2. Make yourself comfortable as you lie on your back on the floor or on a bed—use a pillow at your knees and shoulders if you prefer.

3. While lying on your back, look at the wheel and feel its qualities. When you are ready visualize the wheel standing upright below your feet (or as if you are standing on the wheel). In this position, the wheel will be at a right angle to the floor.

4. Bring the wheel up through your body and allow yourself to feel the energies of it as it travels the length of your body from your feet to the 10th or Lahun chakra. Hold the wheel there. If a wheel feels 'stuck' anywhere, continue to feel the quality of the wheel until it moves freely.

5. When you are ready look at and study the next wheel. Feel how this wheel connects and integrates with the previous wheel. Now visualize this wheel traveling up through your body until it reaches the Lahun chakra. Once again hold it there and continue to the next wheel. Continue until the sequence is complete.

6. When you have completed the sequence you may get up. Remember the sacredness of these wheels and that each wheel is a representation of an actual being.

Note: A sequence may be the 4 Wheels of Inner Peace or the 13 Wheels of Manifestation of Mastery. See the section on the Self Wheels for more information on how the sequences of the 144 Wheels can be completed.

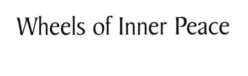
Wheels of Inner Peace

Delighting in the Flow of Change

1

Living in the Light of Complete Self-honesty

2

Living in Perfect Harmonious Inner Integration

3

Finding a Cherishing Inner Home

4

Wheels of Manifestation of Mastery

(Also known as the Wheels of the Goddess Archetypes)

Letting Our Light Shine to the Fullest

1

Expecting Miracles with Hearts of Hope

2

Acknowledging Our Divine Heritage
as Creations of the Infinite

3

Embracing our Divine Perfection

4

Seeing Our Beauty and Majesty Reflected in Nature

5

Knowing All Lives Within Us

6

Claiming All Knowledge and Effortless Knowing

7

Living in the Sovereignty of Self-Expression

8

Taking Full Responsibility for the Quality of Each Moment

9

Living with the Glory of Elegance

10

Pleasing Our Hearts First, that Giving May Come from Fullness

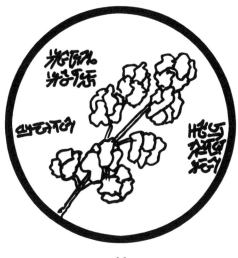

11

Dedicating our Lives to Being the Embodiment of Immortal Glory

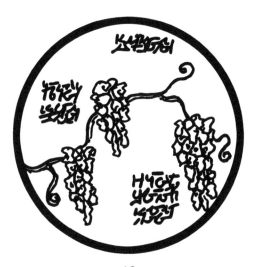

12

Living Each Moment Majestically

13

The Self Wheels

A wheel is a visual image conveying non-cognitive, sacred and empowering information. They are similar to gateways through which specific healing frequencies are drawn and are power sources in the same way that a holy object is or like a mandala.

They are alive and as we work with them they provide us with deep insights into the vastness and wealth of our own being, reminding us of all that we are.

Wheels used in sequence build upon each other and tell a story. Portions of the story make an equation. The equations themselves add up to an overall equation for the 144, which is Adoration in Action. The complete 144 wheels may be integrated in one session or they may be worked with in a number of shorter sequences that each provides a unique alchemical equation.

The individual sequences are as follows and they all start with the first wheel.

Wheels 1–3   –   Powerful Fluid Transfiguration to a Higher Order

Wheels 1–7   –   Energetic Infusion of Enthusiasm

Wheels 1–12   –   Self-Empowerment through Individuality Expressed

Wheels 1–20   –   Interactive Creativity

Wheels 1–33   –   Self-Evident Truth and Transparency

Wheels 1–54   –   Self-Discovered Perfection

Wheels 1–72   –   Choices of Infinite Perfection

Wheels 1–96   –   Delighted Journey of Discovery

Wheels 1–144 –   Adoration in Action

Mystical practices have a beginning and a closure. If you stop in the middle of a sequence without finishing, it leaks resources and energy. For this reason it is important that you always complete each sequence.

The Self Wheels bring transfiguration and creation and move the person's body into the stage of immortality. Working with them on a daily basis maximizes their effects.

To access the information contained within the wheels at a deeper level you may place your hands on the wheels or run your hand across them—the left hand is receptive and the right hand promotes understanding.

The Self Wheels

Wheel of Adoration of the Infinite

1

Wheel of Highly Refined Frequency and Light

2

Wheel of Ultimate Refinement of Life

3

Wheel of Passionate Exploration

4

Wheel of Self-Exploration

5

Wheel of Gratification in Beingness

6

Wheel of Self-Courage

7

Wheel of Self-Sufficiency

8

Wheel of Self-Knowledge

9

Wheel of Self-Gratitude

10

Wheel of Self-Praise

11

Wheel of Self-Celebration

12

Wheel of Self-Beauty

13

Wheel of Self-Grace

14

Wheel of Self-Sustenance

15

Wheel of Integrated Oneness

16

Wheel of Fire Within

17

Wheel of Self-Truth

18

Wheel of Self-Trust

19

Wheel of Self-Generated Resources

20

Wheel of Entrained Frequency

21

Wheel of Innocence

22

Wheel of Purity

23

Wheel of Adoration in Action

24

Wheel of Regeneration

25

Wheel of Self-Respect

26

Wheel of Self-Directed Desires of the Heart

27

Wheel of Joy in Creation

28

Wheel of Self-Mastery in Action

29

Wheel of Self-Seeing Perfection

30

Wheel of Compassionate Understanding

31

Wheel of Self-Confidence

32

Wheel of Self-Acceptance

33

Wheel of Clarity

34

Wheel of Self-Belief

35

Wheel of Self-Determination

36

Wheel of Interconnectedness

37

Wheel of Self-Motivation

38

Wheel of Pristine Coexistence with Nature

39

Wheel of Self-Accomplishment

40

Wheel of Self-Love in Doingness

41

Wheel of Self-Light in Beingness

42

Wheel of Self-Perception

43

Wheel of Unlimited Access to Knowledge

44

Wheel of Experiential Knowledge

45

Wheel of Self-Dignity

46

Wheel of Fluidity in Mastery

47

Wheel of Self-Discovery

48

Wheel of Devoted Service to the Infinite

49

Wheel of Appreciation of Self-Perfection

50

Wheel of Appreciating Self in External Beauty

51

Wheel of Plentiful Supply

52

Wheel of Appreciating Beauty

53

Wheel of Self-Guidance

54

Wheel of Self-Acknowledgement

55

Wheel of Self-Generated Focus in Life

56

Wheel of Peaceful Desires of the Heart

57

Wheel of Balance in Motion

58

Wheel of Alliances with Infinite Intent

59

Wheel of Self-Appreciation

60

Wheel of Self-Responsibility

61

Wheel of Self-Reliance

62

Wheel of Acknowledging Self-Contributions

63

Wheel of Seeing the Value of All Life

64

Wheel of Unified Fields

65

Wheel of Exponential Growth

66

Wheel of Self-Awareness

67

Wheel of Birthing New Paradigms

68

Wheel of Self-Empowerment

69

Wheel of Purification through Gratitude

70

Wheel of Luminous Living

71

Wheel of Self-Recognition of Uniqueness

72

Wheel of Integrated Sub-personalities

73

Wheel of Embracing Life

74

Wheel of Inclusiveness

75

Wheel of Self-Purity

76

Wheel of Enthusiastic Surrender to the Now

77

Wheel of Self-Nurturing

78

Wheel of Self-Stability through Faith

79

Wheel of Self-Assurance through Humility

80

Wheel of Listening with the Heart

81

Wheel of Delighted Self-Expression

82

Wheel of Self-Encouragement

83

Wheel of Moving Horizons

84

Wheel of Cooperative Endeavors

85

Wheel of Communion with Nature

86

Wheel of Exploration of Self through Others

87

Wheel of Acknowledging Self-Divinity

88

Wheel of Interpretative Dance

89

Wheel of Appreciative Awareness of Details

90

Wheel of Efficient Use of Resources

91

Wheel of Humble Assimilation of New Potential

92

Wheel of Countless Achievements

93

Wheel of Expanded Aspirations

94

Wheel of Deepening Experiences

95

Wheel of Fluidly Shifting Consciousness

96

Wheel of Self-Wisdom

97

Wheel of Self-Assessment

98

Wheel of Simplicity of Choices

99

Wheel of Freedom from Nostalgia of the Past

100

Wheel of Collaboration to Do Life-Enhancing Work

101

Wheel of Creating New Memories

102

Wheel of Boundless Growth through Grace

103

Wheel of Individual Relationship with the Infinite

104

Wheel of Abundant Living

105

Wheel of Joyful Journey of Discovery

106

Wheel of Emotional Self-Fulfillment

107

Wheel of New Creations

108

Wheel of All-Encompassing Presence

109

Wheel of Releasing Duty

110

Wheel of Releasing Resistance

111

Wheel of Authenticity

112

Wheel of Self-Manifested Intent

113

Wheel of One Heart Mind

114

Wheel of Pristine Creations

115

Wheel of Imaginative Expression

116

Wheel of Expanding Inner Sight

117

Wheel of Heaven on Earth

118

Wheel of Acknowledging Earth's Divinity

119

Wheel of Communion with the Infinite

120

Wheel of Complete Release

121

Wheel of Deeper Understanding of the Infinite

122

Wheel of Dissolving Obsolete Patterns

123

Wheel of Unlimited Learning

124

Wheel of Dissolving Dysfunctionality

125

Wheel of Complete Trust in Divine Order

126

Wheel of Flowering

127

Wheel of Honoring Diversity

128

Wheel of Oneness with the Infinite

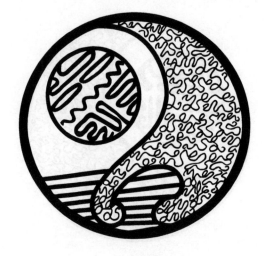

129

Wheel of Full Emotional Expression

130

Wheel of Eternal Life

131

Wheel of Creating Sacred Space

132

Wheel of Physical Manifestation

133

Wheel of Restoration to Magical Life

134

Wheel of Mastery of Alchemy

135

Wheel of Becoming Divine Architects

136

Wheel of Instant Access to Infinite Knowledge

137

Wheel of Restoration of Magical Kingdoms

138

Wheel of Dissolving Stagnant Boundaries

139

Wheel of Dissolving Programming

140

Wheel of Perfect Harmony

141

Wheel of Limitless Creativity

142

Wheel of Unobstructive Vision

143

Wheel of Everlasting Guidance by the Infinite

144

The One Wheel that Contains All

The Wheel of Higher Consciousness

Closing for Kaanish Belvaspata

What greater gift can we give another than the gift of enlightenment? Through ages of being in stages of deep forgetfulness, called the Great Fall, the cosmos has emerged into a state of Ascension. Growth used to come through opposition and insights lay hidden in the adversities of our lives.

This is no longer so. Growth now comes through grace and support: one of the many reasons so many sacred tools are being given to man. Effortless knowing has replaced delving for insights through the painful experiences of our lives. The greater the service we render, the more profound the enlightenment to us.

Kaanish Belvaspata is the vehicle to make a profound impact not only on others but also on the practitioners who use it. Each time it is used, it brings us closer to personal mastery; that state of being in which we see from all perspectives at once and have the option to function from the silence of the mind.

May we receive it with gratitude, acknowledging with honor and respect its holy origin as a gift from the Infinite Being.

In love, praise and gratitude,

Almine

Book III

Belvaspata for the
Song of Self

Introduction to Belvaspata for
The Song of the Self

Pain is caused by the illusion of separation. Separation is caused when parts of the body do not emit their harmonious frequencies — do not sing their song. Unsung songs lie like shadows in the etheric body. This body of Belvaspata is specifically designed to release the hold of separation caused by unexpressed frequencies.

~ Almine

Belvaspata of The Song of the Self promotes the healing of bodily inflammation by resolving internal emotional conflicts.

About the Wheels

Higher life of increased consciousness uses eight directions: North, East, South, West, Above, Below, Within and Without. These also represent the stages of evolution[1] all life moves through. They are also expressed as the eight sub-personalities[2] of higher awareness.

---

1 See *Journey to the Heart of God.*
2 See *The Lemurian Science of Peace.*

345

The first eight wheels represent these eight directions. There are no angels to call to represent them.

These are in actuality vast rivers of sub-quantum particles that lie throughout the macrocosm and manifest within man (the microcosm) as sub-personalities.

~ Almine

Almine has further explained that these eight structural components of existence are too vast to be represented by angelic beings. The remaining 21 wheels lead us beyond directions to an existence of no opposites.

They are the representation of the spheres found in the Flower of Life pattern—the template of life. The divisions of the spheres are caused by unexpressed frequencies which this body of Belvaspata restores.

How to Use the Wheels of The Song of Self

- Start the session for Belvaspata of The Song of Self with a period of expansion for 5 – 10 minutes or as long as you feel guided.
- Sign (draw) the sigils of the 8 Wheels that represent the Directions once while saying their name. Only draw the sigil within the center.
- Sign the sigils within the center of the 21 Wheels of the Songs while saying their name which is located at the bottom of the wheel. Then glance at the sigil at the top of the wheel — this sigil is not drawn.
- Finish the session by drawing the sigils of Love, Praise and Gratitude over the heart area of the person or yourself.
- All levels of Belvaspata masters may use The Song of Self. It can be done for self or for another.
- If you wish to do Belvaspata For the Song of Self along with another form of Belvaspata, the Song of Self must always be done first.

Note: There are no angels, but the sigil at the top in the rim has a very sacred purpose. It connects with the same tone within the Infinite and activates within the person the Song of Self Belvaspata that they are receiving. When a specific note is struck on a piano, the same note vibrates elsewhere on the piano. This is the principle of harmonic resonance that applies in this instance.

The Wheels Representing the Directions

Kersanach Suvahesbi
Uniformity

1

Pluhavat Una-Arasvabi
Diversity Within Uniformity

2

Kilsavat Arasklat
Diversity

3

Trubarut Arat-Prihabi
Unity Within Diversity

4

Kisanahut-Alasvi
Diversity Within Unity (Autonomy)

5

Erek-Trave Ninaves
Self-sovereignty

6

Kluvas-Priha Usvabit
Absolute Oneness

7

Nenesh-Klasve Ersklavit
Diversity Within Oneness

8

The Wheels of the Songs

The Song of Self

1

The Song of Light

2

The Song of Unfolding Newness

3

The Song of Life

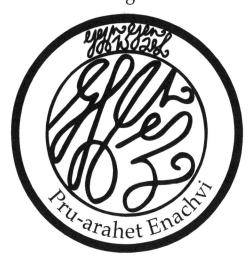

4

The Song of Being an Instrument of Art

5

The Song of Civilization

6

The Song of Absolution

7

The Song of Indiscriminate Appreciation

8

The Song of the Body

Kirsitaa-herechvi

9

The Song of Knowledge

Ketre-misuvet

10

The Song of Abundant Plenitude

11

The Song of the Earth

12

The Song of Uncompromising Freedom

13

The Song of Inclusiveness

14

The Song of the Original Ones

Tarech Besba

15

The Song of Humanity

Puhu-anet-skleva

16

The Song of Relationship

Mananach-selhavi

17

The Song of Full Interpretation and Expression of the Nuances of Indivisible Existence

Éte-anik Peleva

18

The Song of Humor

19

The Song of Dynamically Balanced Androgyny

20

The Song of Existing Beyond Opposites

21

A Flower of Life Sphere

The divisions of the Flower of Life Sphere are formed by suppressed frequencies. Belvaspata for The Song of the Self heals these divisions within us at a cellular level.

The divisions of the Flower of Life Sphere are formed by suppressed frequencies. Beirspata for The Song of the Self hold these divisions within it at a cellular level.

Book IV

Braamish Ananu Belvaspata
The Belvaspata of the Gods

Introduction to Braamish Ananu

Belvaspata of the Gods

The translation of the Holy Records of Ananu, ancient tablets that preceded the Earth finding her way into this solar system, reveal the following:

- There are two species that appear as man — humanity and the Ancient Ones. The primary difference lies in the DNA.

- The human DNA has had 12 strands, of which 2 are visible and 10 are not. The Ancient Ones have 12 clusters of DNA strands, of which 10 are invisible.

- The major lightworkers of the earth are the Ancient Ones and seem as men because they have forgotten who they are. They have assumed the limiting belief systems of humanity.

- The Original Ones, or Ancient Ones, were created eons before humanity and dwelled in a different plane of existence that was more magnetic. Their memories are held in this alternate reality (a horizontal cosmic wheel) where they dwell as well.

- The vertical cosmic wheel is where form began. It is where light and sound split from having been one, and where time began. Time is the movement of emotion based on desire.

- The movement of the vertical cosmos creates linear time. By bringing a higher form of emotion into manifestation, ones not based on desire but on the recognition of what is, we can bring an end to this movement and thus to linear time.

- This creates a 'language' that can be understood in both realities so that the Ancient Ones can merge the two different realities by healing their own schism.

- The words Braamish Ananu mean Holy or Divine Androgynous Gods. Pain has come through separation; through oneness, all life flourishes. This Belvaspata of Divinity creates a timeless existence beyond mortal boundaries for both the one who gives and the one who receives it, thus promoting the illumination of inner divinity.

Preparations for working with Braamish Ananu Belvaspata

In order to prepare for Braamish Ananu Belvaspata, the High Alchemy of Belvaspata, please follow these guidelines:

- You must have at least a Level I Belvaspata initiation.
- A full 30 days daily practice of Kaanish Belvaspata is necessary before starting to work with Braamish Ananu. At least one level should be performed each day and all levels should be done consecutively. Integration of all the wheels following Level 5, is to be done at least once during the 30 days.
- It is also suggested that you spend some time with the Emotions of Recognition and the Rays of Realization of Motionless Luminosity to feel and understand their qualities. You may use your hand by moving it across the sigil to enhance your experience — the left hand for receptivity and the right for understanding.

The purpose of doing Kaanish Belvaspata is to prepare and purify you, your home, your work and your environment. Following this preparation you may use Braamish Belvaspata on yourself or on another.

It may be used on its own or as part of a fuller session of Belvaspata. It can also be combined with any of the other Specialty Belvaspata modalities.

Using Braamish Ananu Belvaspata for self or for another individual

1. Open the session with an expansion process and hold the expanded awareness for as long as you feel is appropriate. For example, 5–10 minutes may be sufficient.

2. Proceed with Braamish Ananu Belvaspata. Draw the sigils for the pairs of Emotions of Recognition and the Rays of Motionless Luminosity in the air and call upon the angels as you look at their sigils.

3. Always close the session by signing the sigils for love, praise and gratitude over the heart area as this materializes the healing intentions and pulls awareness in.

The Emotions of Recognition

1a. Plenitude: The recognition that I have all

Esplet-uresva-arunich   **Angel: Sperabit-arachva**

1b. Omni-presence: The recognition that I am all

Keseret-michba-henachvi   **Angel: Eseva-anasvi**

2a. Rapture: The recognition of Infinite existence in stillness

Arskra-minuvech-haraset   **Angel: Minaruch-sebatu**

2b. Reverential Existence: The recognition of Mundane Sacredness

Pilhivat-uresklave-minuvash   **Angel: Kirseva-arasklave**

3a. Omni-perspective: The recognition of simplicity in complexity

Bri-harasbak-unekvi   **Angel: Pliharabak-setvi**

3b. Timelessness: The recognition of the fullness of all in the moment

Nesva-erstahur-minakvi   **Angel: Misavek-patre-hur**

4a. Creating Absolute Truth: The recognition of existence as a devotional prayer

Karsana-mishata-bluhavek   **Angel: Machte-minusat-varesbi**

4b. Fulfilled Contentment: The recognition of the unfolding wonderment of existence

Kaarasech-varuspavi-menesut   **Angel: Petrehur-asanavi**

5a. *Awakened Awareness*: The recognition of meticulous caring

Pletevra-sasu-anat-huve   **Angel: Pluhu-aret-pretlva**

5b. *Fluid Vastness*: The recognition of dynamic balance in expression

Kenavish-mitreva-uhanesh   **Angel: Pahur-plekba-nenuklish**

6a. *Supported Expression:* The recognition of limitless supply of resources

Plihararak-nechta-uves   **Angel: Kaashanit-hespava**

6b. *Deep Peace*: The recognition of the self as the only being in existence

Ke-esech-aasena-blavahut   **Angel: Kirit-vartaa-menuvech**

7a. Effortless Knowing: The recognition of indivisible existence

Kurasta-uva-anastat   **Angel: Achnet-usevesvi**

7b. Unchangeable Perfection: The recognition of new revelations

Mechpa-uhururespi-aravach   **Angel: Niseret-arakba-
                                                          minuvish**

8a. Carefree Surrender: The recognition of the impeccability of
timing of the unfolding revelations of Oneness

Nenklesh-viraspa-uhur   **Angel: Nechti-ubrava-selvavi**

8b. Harmonic Resonance: The recognition of the perfection of
expressions of diverse consciousness

Esseve-nusklave-pruhanit   **Angel: Kerene-asavat-
                                                          unesvi**

9a. *Lighthearted Eternal Presence:* The recognition of fluid, eternal existence

Nash-pru-aret-viraveski

Angel: Arachvraba-nunasut

9b. *Comforting Presence*: The recognition of floating on the calm waves of existence

Belerut-aravesvi-menusat

Angel: Taruch-beleska

10a. *Perpetual Freshness of Expression:* The recognition of countless possibilities of eternal existence

Mechpa-barurit-askantave

Angel: Urach-virisat

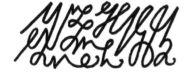

10b. *Eternal Fulfillment*: The recognition of the complete equity of existence

Brihanut-uvechstre-aranas

Angel: Nechba-uhuru-ruspave

11a. *Supreme Elegance:* The recognition of infinite diversity of beauty

Achne-birestak-ufreve-minasvi

Angel: Kaanech-harestat-vereblut

11b. *Confidence of Purity:* The recognition of the benevolence of unfolding life

Bluhablat-ereckvi-sta-urat

Angel: Eskleve-miresh-esete

12a. *Humorous Conjunction*: The recognition of Infinite bliss

Pilestreve-hinusat-aresvi

Angel: Kaa-ahanish-ustrechvi

12b. *Transient Expression of Indivisible Form:* The recognition of form as the ever-renewed vehicle of Infinite Intent

Kesetre-hubavich-uresve

Angel: Pruhavat-nenuchvi

The 16 Rays of Realization
of Motionless Luminosity

1. The realization that knowledge binds us to a matrix, whereas experiential awareness sets us free.

Nichpa-erestu   **Angel: Kira-virablu**

---

2. The realization that since all is eternally new, all is unknowable.

Neseracu-eleshvu   **Angel: Kisel-haras-vi**

---

3. The realization that all knowledge is obsolete. What is obsolete can be termed 'density'.

Plehe-ustarat   **Angel: Kevenurasat**

---

4. The realization that any reference point is an illusion when all is in a state of flux.

Mechpa-reresuch   **Angel: Sitre-here-such**

5. The realization that our desire to hold onto experience as knowledge forms linear time through creating the procession of moments.

Kiravech-stuhavet   **Angel: Plihat-serve-tu**

6. The realization that perpetual rejuvenation is the nature of existence and is the result of having no reference point.

Mesetu-arsavat   **Angel: Mesetach-bilevit**

7. The realization that life is a trapped existence on a two-dimensional screen. It is formed by belief systems and world views.

Klasanut-esevach   **Angel: Mesenach-pretevit**

8. The realization that the rotation of the disc of life is caused by desire-based emotions and moving light.

Kerserut-aravach   **Angel: Sevetach-ruraklat**

9. The realization that moving light comes from anticipating the future. This perpetuates the past.

Plehet-arasku   **Angel: Karanat-pirenesvi**

10. The realization that motionless existence is no more real
than the disc of life. They are opposites and anything that has an
opposite is not real.

Akravit-vileshpli   **Angel: Peretut-akrava**

11. The realization that achieving stillness within movement of
light comes from the trusting acceptance of effortless knowing.

Naskave-skrihuvat   **Angel: Netrevit-uharavas**

12. The realization that movement in motionless luminosity comes
from the rapture of aware experience.

Neshti-uklat-par-ve   **Angel: Virichpa-heleshvi**

13. The realization that the need to justify comes from the distorted emotion of guilt. This created the need to understand and the tool of intelligence arose.

Mirechpa-ersatu   **Angel: Kenesta-plihuvech**

14. The realization that the cosmic law of compensation permits no inequality, even though we cannot see it from our perspective. This sets us free from guilt and the need to justify our existence.

Sarsut-menechsta   **Angel: Kuharet-mirchspa**

15. The realization that by balancing the masculine (balancing light), and by balancing the feminine (balancing frequency), the body becomes a supplier of energy rather than a taker.

Kenevech-surspa   **Angel: Nenechsut-u-arech**

16. The realization that by balancing the elements of existence we live from the center point of the two axes – the place of oneness, the inner sanctum.

Kenesut-aruvech   **Angel: Nenes-arsava**

These combined Rays of Light equal:

The contented rapture of aware experience

Closing Sigils

Praise

Love

Gratitude

Appendices

Appendix I

Gas Discharge Visualization to Determine the Effectiveness of Healing Methods

By Dr Sabina DeVita

A study was initiated in the presence of the healer Almine to ascertain visible and scientific measures of changes on the biological systems of a small group of subjects. The Gas Discharge Visualization (GDV) Bioelectrography camera was used.

About the Bioelectrography Camera

The Bioelectrography camera measures the human energy field and allows us to detect and monitor changes in the subtle energy fields of the individual. The energy field is a cosmic blueprint and use of this technology was most appropriate in monitoring the participants in this study.

The camera is the most advanced comprehensive full-body imaging device available on the market today, used and developed by

Dr. Konstantin Korotkov, a leading Russian physicist internationally renowned for the pioneering research he conducted on the human energy field over approximately the last 20 years.

The system allows for direct, real-time photos and videos of the entire energy field of a human as well as other organisms and materials. The information is extracted by computer software that measures brightness, size, fractality and other parameters of the energy field. It is a unique system, distinctive from that used in Kirilian photography.

The photographs can give information about the psychological, emotional and physical condition of the subject. This aura-imaging technique is especially useful in showing changes in the subtle energy distribution around the human body before and after any experience.

The Study

The principal author, Dr. DeVita, conducted all testing of subjects, pre and post, over a 6-day period. The study consisted of a small group of subjects who were subjected to specific healing conducted by Almine. The testing methodology was based on individual GDV analysis of psychological/emotional/physical states. Post- and pre-GDV photography was taken to observe the effectiveness of the healing.

Dr. DeVita was personally trained by Dr. Korotkov in Canada in October 2001. More advanced training was received in July 2002 in St. Petersburg, Russia. She received an International Certificate for her presentation of clinical data to the VI Scientific Congress and for her active participation in hands-on training workshops.

About Dr. Konstantin Korotkov, inventor of the technology used in this study

Dr. Krotokov is Professor of Computer Science and Biophysics at Saint-Petersburg Federal University of Informational Technologies, Mechanics and Optics and Professor of Research in Saint Petersburg Academy of Physical Culture. He holds 12 patents on biophysics inventions and is the author of more than 90 papers on physics and biology published in leading Russian and international journals. He has written multiple books, published in Russian, English and Italian. The titles include: *Life after Life: Experiments and Ideas on After-Death Changes of Kirilian Pictures,* 1998, NY Backbone Publishing Co., and *Aura and Consciousness: New Stage of Scientific Understanding,* 1999, St. Petersburg, 'Kultura'. Dr. Korotkov is also President of the International Union of Medical and Applied Bioelectrography.

Analysis and Interpretation of GDV Information

The Gas Discharge Visualization camera created by Dr. Konstantin Korotkov is the first device in the world that measures the distribution of the energy level of biological objects (energy geomeo kinesis). It is being used for medical diagnosis in many medical facilities.

This technique is based on the visual observation or registration on a photo film of gas discharge fluorescence as it appears close to the surface of the investigated subject, placing it into a high intensity electromagnetic field. Using computer software, analysis is estimated by means of non-linear mathematics and data-mining methods developed by Russian scientists. It has been successfully trialed in Russia, England, Germany, Slovenia, the United States and is acknowledged in many other countries.

Healthy Aura

The field of a healthy active person is dense, uniform and has smooth changes of color from the blue spectrum through the orange to the yellow. Both psychological and physical profiles of each subject were taken before and after the healing sessions.

Disturbances

Holes, gaps, heterogeneities and outbursts in the aura are indicators of disturbances in the energy field. They point to disorders on mental, functional or organ levels, showing a direct link to the organ system indicated on the Beogram (aura picture). Left and right side projections of the image show disturbances that relate to both logical cerebral and right intuitive hemispheres and right and left sides of the body.

Gaps or breaks in the psychological/emotional profile represent leakage of energy and the individual is most likely experiencing a number of powerful symptoms. The images of the Beograms help us to decode an individual's main psycho-emotional state and denote the relationship between the organs and the psyche.

Old Chinese texts link rage with liver damage, worry with spleen damage. Cord-like structures appear to enter and exit the body, often indicating attachments between people via intense emotions coupled with thoughts of fear or worry.

Brief Interpretations of 3 Subjects from this Study

Subjects 1, 2 and 3 are presented here both before and after their healing sessions. All three displayed gaps, holes and cords plus irregular energy fields. The pictures and diagrams included display the definitive improvement after the healing. The 'before' GDV Kirlian picture outlines the disturbed energy field. The 'after' image displays the bio-energetic change and the significant effectiveness of Almine's intervention.

In conclusion, this study shows that the spiritual healing of these 3 individuals as performed by Almine was indeed successful. Similar effects were noted on each of the other participants.

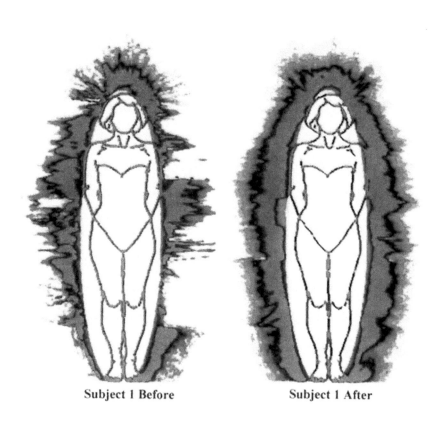

Subject 1 Before   Subject 1 After

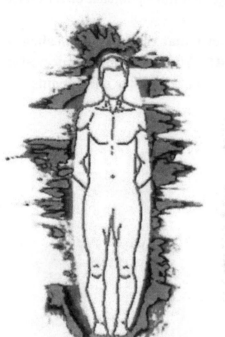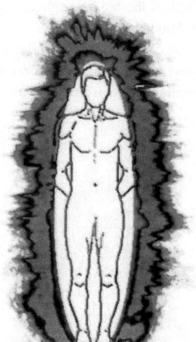

Subject 2 Before   Subject 2 After

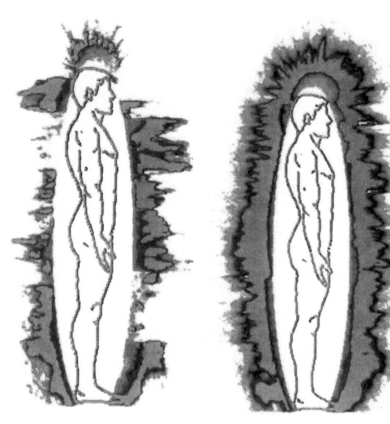

Subject 2 Before

Side View

Subject 2 After

Side View

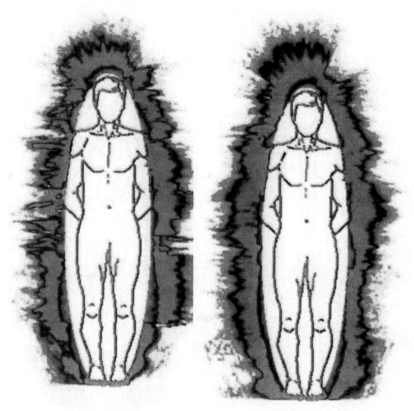

Subject 3 Before   **Subject 3 After**

Appendix II

Guidance for Beginning Healers

by Almine

As our journey of exploring the intricate art of healing and our responsibilities as healers begin, you are urged to remember that the more you grow, the more you will gain from this information. You may, therefore, wish to return to it periodically and re-read portions of it that new layers may reveal themselves to you.

Whether the techniques have a mild or profound effect on those who come to you for assistance will depend largely on how well you have internalized the qualities given in the *Belvaspata* section. Do not heal for the sake of results, so that you can remain unencumbered by the weight of self-reflection. However, you will become more and more aware of how healing frequencies respond to you. This, like the acquisition of any other skill, will grow with practice. The techniques provided give you something with which to practise. The illusion of disease comes in an instant and so can healing, but knowing what to heal and asking the right questions in giving your client guidance is a product of humility, an openness to receiving information and of practice.

It is recommended that beginning healers form free healing circles, as their time is available (evenings and weekends, perhaps) to develop the skills necessary for working with clients. Recognition of the divinity of those who come for assistance, as well as a deep and abiding compassion, can make even a beginning healer effective.

Always be sure you are not in a state of emotional duress and that you have had sufficient food and water. Take time to establish a sacred space and to cleanse it after each client. The work you are doing is holy in that it removes the filters that block the passage of light. Treat your healing room as worship space. Make sure that when your client leaves, they do not encounter disruptive or hostile emotions from others in the building, since they will be wide open and highly sensitive.

We urge healers to study and abide by the laws of the state in which they reside. In many states it is illegal to say, "I heal" and healers have to call themselves healing facilitators. In others it is illegal to touch another person unless you are licensed to do so. A minister's license will enable you to do so legally. They are easy to obtain and can be kept current at little cost. Even though there are homeopathics remedies strong enough to heal disease, it may be necessary to represent them as facilitating healing or as nutritional aids.

Dealing with these sacred healing modalities where the veils between realities become thin and the past and present merge with the future takes great courage. With impeccability as your shield and in a place of balance that has shed the need to impress, your steps will be guided so you may stride forward unafraid to reveal the perfection that dwells in all beings.

Seeing the divinity within ourselves enables us to see it in another. To approach our fellow man as less than divine is to deny the Source of his being. He is an arrow sent forth from the hand of the Infinite, straight and true upon its course. The ancient Norsemen shot flaming arrows into mist to guide their boats safely into the unknown. In the same way we have been sent like flaming arrows to explore the mysteries of the Infinite's Being. All flaming arrows are of equal value to the navigator; some tell him where it is clear to go and others showing where it is not. In the same way within the mystery of the Infinite's Being, all are equal. There is much value in mirroring to the Infinite, through the experience of a life, that which It is not, so It might fully understand that which It is.

Exerting influence on the life of another is a sacred, awesome responsibility. When our fellow man approaches us to ask for help, remember his true identity as a being vast as the cosmos having a human experience and approach him with humility and impeccability. For in helping birth him into an awareness of the infinite possibilities that lie sleeping within his soul, we are helping him find the diamonds of divinity lying hidden in the dust of illusion.

There is great value in opposition and, hidden within the shadows of density, lies the impetus to set us free from mortal boundaries. Without friction, no creature can walk upon the Earth. Nature has designed the opposition that any fetus must overcome to earn the right to life. In truth, opposition strengthens and in a similar manner we strengthen density when we oppose it. We strengthen the shortcomings we suppress and the illness we combat. Challenge yields perception and perception yields power. If we pull the chicken prematurely from the egg, it dies. If we remove a sufferer's pain without assisting him to receive its insights, a great dawn of illumination might die stillborn.

Throughout the cosmos the Infinite has gained in luminosity and power, not by denying the unsolved mystery of 'The Dark' within Its Being, but by including it within the light so it might yield its insights. The greatest service we can render as the One expressing as the many is to remember who we are, for in this memory all is included. The greatest hardships hold within their overcomings the greatest miracles.

As wielders of power, our balance is maintained through constantly remembering that the insights gained in all of life's journeys are of equal value in enriching the One. The vast majority of Creation falls within the realm of that which, from our vantage point, is unknowable. This eliminates the temptation to yield to the compulsion of the left-brain to reduce the infinite to the finite. It stifles the incessant need to know and sets us free from attachment to outcome.

To sow in order to reap gives only the harvest as reward. But to sow like a pilgrim traveling through the land, scattering seeds along the way with no thought of benefit from their eventual fruition is to become an instrument in the hand of the Infinite. We sow, not to reap the benefit, but because the seeds are in our hands and our passage blesses all creatures. As we bless others with the seeds of healing, let us remain unencumbered by self-reflection and unfettered by self-importance. Do not focus on the results of your healing; it is life giving unto life. You are the blessed flute upon which the Infinite plays divine melody. Be assured that, in as much as the soil of the soul is responsive, the seed will grow even if the fruit or flower of its maturity arrives long after you have passed.

The sublime path of being a blessing to mankind, shedding light on dark days, is not for those who pretend ignorance to escape culpability. It is not for those who hide behind false humility, which is simply conceding to the arrogance of another. Instead, it is for men and women willing to let their light increasingly illuminate with the soft flow of hope the darkest corners of the lives they touch. It calls for masters with the innocence of a child, who freely acknowledge their inability to know the infinite plan of wisdom that shapes the lives of their fellow men. Through these masters, the Infinite speaks.

There are those who grasp greedily at every scrap of information, never pausing to incorporate it into their lives. They hoard and store and study knowledge as if by merely knowing it, they can gain power. Book volumes of information cannot enrich those who do not do the work within. Yet a person who has made wisdom their own will find their lives altered by a single phrase. It is to them that I speak. It is my sincere desire to share with healers, through these teachings, the continual stream of knowledge I receive. There is no limit to the knowledge that can be brought forth on this planet, but it must be called through the human heart.

Appendix III

Example of a Belvaspata Certificate

BELVASPATA

HEALING of the HEART

Light and Frequency

~Almine~

GRAND MASTERY LEVEL

is hereby granted to

Granted on:

Grand Master Teacher

Other books by Almine

A Life of Miracles
***Expanded Third Edition* Includes Bonus Belvaspata Section—Mystical Keys to Ascension**
Almine's developing spiritual awareness and abilities from her childhood in South Africa until she emerged as a powerful mystic, to devote her gifts in support of all humanity is traced. Deeply inspiring and unique in its comparison of man's relationship as the microcosm of the macrocosm. *Also available in Spanish.*

Published: 2009, 304 pages, soft cover, 6 x 9, ISBN: 978-1-934070-25-3

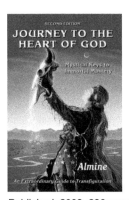

Journey to the Heart of God *Second Edition*
Mystical Keys to Immortal Mastery
Ground-breaking cosmology revealed for the first time, sheds new light on previous bodies of information such as the Torah, the I Ching and the Mayan Zolkien. The explanation of man's relationship as the microcosm as set out in the previous book *A Life of Miracles*, is expanded in a way never before addressed by New Age authors, giving new meaning and purpose to human life. Endorsed by an Astrophysicist from Cambridge University and a former NASA scientist, this book is foundational for readers at all levels of spiritual growth.

Published: 2009, 296 pages, soft cover, 6 x 9, ISBN: 978-1-934070-26-0

The Ring of Truth *Third Edition*
Sacred Secrets of the Goddess
As man slumbers in awareness, the nature of his reality has altered forever. As one of the most profound mystics of all time, Almine explains this dramatic shift in cosmic laws that is changing life on earth irrevocably. A powerful healing modality is presented to compensate for the changes in laws of energy, healers have traditionally relied upon. The new principles of beneficial white magic and the massive changes in spiritual warriorship are meticulously explained.

Published: 2009, 256 pages, soft cover, 6 x 9, ISBN: 978-1-934070-28-4

Other books by Almine

Arubafirina *Third Edition*
The Book of Fairy Magic

This book is most certainly a milestone in the history of mysticism throughout the ages. It is the product of a rare and unprecedented event in which Almine, acknowledged as the leading mystic of our time, was granted an exceptional privilege. For one week in November 2006 she was invited to enter the fairy realms and gather the priceless information for this book. The result is a tremendous treasure trove of knowledge and interdimensional color photos.

Published: 2011, 340 pages, soft cover, 6 x 9, ISBN: 978-1-936926-32-9

Opening the Doors of Heaven *Second Edition*
Revelations of the Mysteries of Isis

Through a time-travel tunnel, linking Ireland and Egypt, Isis sent a small group of masters to prepare for the day when her mysteries would once again be released to the world to restore balance and enhance life.

They established the Order of the White Rose to guard the sacred objects and the secrets of Isis. In an unprecedented event heralding the advent of a time of light, these mysteries are released for the first time.

Published: 2009, 312 pages, soft cover, 6 x 9 ISBN: 978-1-934070-31-4

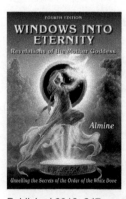

Windows Into Eternity *Fourth Edition*
Revelations of the Mother Goddess

Through an unprecedented series of revelations, profound, upgraded material has been received by the Seer Almine to produce this powerful new edition.
This book provides unparalleled insight into ancient mysteries. The Seer Almine, an internationally recognized mystic and teacher, reveals the hidden laws of existence. Transcending reason and delivering visionary expansion, this metaphysical masterpiece explores the origins of life as recorded in the Holy Libraries. The release of information from these ancient libraries is a priceless gift to humankind.

Published 2013, 347 pages, soft cover, 6 x 9, ISBN 978-1-936926-68-8

Other books by Almine

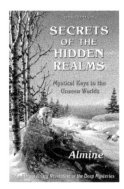

Secrets of the Hidden Realms, *Third Edition*
Mystical Keys to the Unseen Worlds
This remarkable book delves into mysteries few mystics have ever revealed. It gives in detail: *The practical application of the goddess mysteries • Secrets of the angelic realms • The maps, alphabets, numerical systems of Lemuria, Atlantis, and the Inner Earth • The Atlantean calender, accurate within 5 minutes • The alphabet of the Akashic libraries. Secrets of the Hidden Realms* is a truly amazing bridge across the chasm that has separated humanity for eons from unseen realms.

Published: 2011, 412 pages, soft cover, 6 x 9, ISBN: 978-1-936926-38-1

Secrets of Dragon Magic, The Sacred Fires of the Hadji-ka
This extraordinary record of the philosophy and practices of dragon magic is unmatched in its depth of knowledge and powerful delivery. From the *Sacred Records of the Hadji-ka*, kept by the dragons of Avondar, the secrets of Kundalini are revealed, designed to restore the innate, natural magical abilities of man lost by the separation of the spinal column and the pranic tube. The reader is swept along on a profound and mystical journey that pushes perception beyond mortal boundaries. Almine's infallible ability to empower her reading audience is clearly felt throughout the pages of this book.

Published: 2013, 373 pages, soft cover, 6 x 9, $24.95, ISBN: 978-1-936926-56-5

Handbook for Healer
The Healing Wisdom of the Seer Almine
Handbook for Healers is an invaluable tool for anyone interested in self-healing or the healing of others. It offers both practical and spiritual guidance gleaned from the globally acclaimed Seer Almine's advice to her students during the past decade. It reveals vital information on rejuvenating the body and understanding its communication through the language of pain, and many more empowering insights.

Published 2013, 648 pages, 6 x 9, ISBN 978-1-936926-44-2

Other books by Almine

Belvaspata, Angel Healing, Volume II
Healing through Oneness Plus: The Integrated Use of Fragrance Alchemy.
Whether you are a beginner or an experienced master of the miraculous healing modality of Belvaspata, this comprehensive guide is an information rich handbook that will serve as your most valuable tool – a compendium of information for everything you need to know to establish yourself as a practitioner of this miraculous healing modality of the angels. Belvaspata Volume II includes "The Integrated Use of Fragrance Alchemy," which delivers the method to obtain wellness of the emotional, mental and physical bodies through the combined use of Belvaspata, the alchemy of fragrance and the Atlantean Healing Sigils.

Published: 2012, 467 pages, soft cover, 6 x 9, ISBN: 978-1-936926-40-4

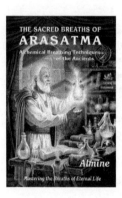

The Sacred Breaths of Arasatma
Alchemcial Breathing Techniques of the Ancients
The Arasatma Breathing Technique was used by ancient mystics to activate the unused portion of the pranic tube for fuller self-expression and inner peace. A fully cleared and active pranic tube is the gateway to a magical life. Also, these breathing techniques aid in the restoration of the subtle, etheric functions of the body and senses. This allows the practitioner to access other dimensions and prolongs an eternal life of graceful unfolding. This book doesn't only share the first 3 levels of this powerful breathing technique but for the first time also publicly shares 3 follow-up levels to those who wish to continue their journey with this powerful transformative tool.

Published: 2013, 363 pages, soft cover, 6 x 9, $34.95, ISBN: 978-1-936926-64-0

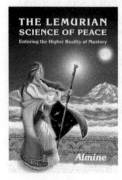

Lemurian Science of Peace
Entering the Higher Realities of Mastery
This remarkable book delivers the best of both worlds: Deep metaphysical concepts alternating with easy steps for their application. Both serious students of the mysteries, and casual readers seeking easy guidance for masterful living, should find what they are looking for.

Published 2013, 332 pages, soft cover, 6 x 9, $24.95, ISBN: 978-1-936926-89-3

Music by Almine

Children of the Sun

Music from the Known Planets (Re-mastered and re-titled
version of the Interstellar Sound Elixirs) The beautiful
interstellar sound elixirs received and sung by Almine.

Price $9.95 MP3 Download
$14.95 CD

Labyrinth of the Moon

Music from the Hidden Planets (Re-titled version of the
Sound Elixirs of the Hidden Planets) All the vocals in these
elixirs are received and sung in the moment by Almine

Price $9.95 MP3 Download
$14.95 CD

Jubilation – Songs of Praise

Music from around the world to lift the heart and inspire the
listener. The extraordinary mystical quality of the music, and
the exquisite clarity of Almine's voice, creates the ambient
impression of being in the presence of angels.

Price $9.95 MP3 Download
$14.95 CD

Additional Products by Almine

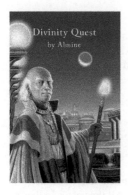

Divinity Quest

Through ages of existence of cycles of life, death and ascension, there are those great lights on Earth who have felt the deep anguish of knowing that the reality of man is not their own; that a higher reality beckons. Almine has laid down a map for the magnificent journey home to the greater reality of godhood.

Divinity Quest is a physical card deck for divination and DNA activation. It's an easy yet profound tool, enabling the remembrance and activation of your divine origin in daily life.

Price $34.95

Elfin Quest

The 60 cards of *Elfin Quest* have many important roles to play in your life. They are not only a source of daily guidance and inspiration, but also a sacred tool to evolve consciousness and facilitate healing.

The healing protocol included with the card deck, allows the life force to flow unimpeded through the spine to increase the vitality present in various parts of the body.

Elfin Quest is a powerful and life altering tool, brought to you by the leading mystic of our time.

Price $34.95

9 781936 926923